(continued from front flap)

She has known many places and many people. Her story takes us from the small, sheltering Midwest community where she was raised to wartime Washington, D.C., the opulent north shore of Long Island, the villages of the Hopi Indians, and to Paris, Zanzibar, Egypt, and the Holy Land with numerous stops in between. We are introduced to such internationally famous people as His Highness the late Aga Khan, Princess Grace of Monaco, Terence Cardinal Cooke, Billy and Ruth Graham, as well as to the countless warm friends, colleagues, and acquaintances who have enriched her everyday life.

In this book Mrs. Whitney comments thoughtfully on the special challenges of today—among them the youth culture, the demands for social relevancy, and ecumenism. She also presents her insights on such fundamental human concerns as marriage, death, and how to lead a truly abundant and purposeful life.

INVITATION TO JOY is an intimate and lively autobiography, radiating the unique power of God's transforming love.

INVITATION TO JOY

ELEANOR SEARLE WHITNEY

Invitation to Joy

A PERSONAL STORY

1817

HARPER & ROW, PUBLISHERS

New York, Evanston, San Francisco
London

Selections from the Bible are from the following translations:

The Holy Bible, Authorized King James Version (AV).
The Holy Bible, Revised Standard Version (RSV).
The New English Bible (NEB).
The New Testament in Modern English, translated by J. B. Phillips.
*Good News for Modern Man, The New Testament in Today's English
    Version* (TEV).
Living Letters: The Paraphrased Epistles, edited by K. N. Taylor.
A Contemporary Translation (ACT).
The Jerusalem Bible (JB).

INVITATION TO JOY. *Copyright © 1971 by Eleanor Searle Whitney. All rights
reserved. Printed in the United States of America. No part of this book may
be used or reproduced in any manner whatsoever without written permission
except in the case of brief quotations embodied in critical articles and
reviews. For information address Harper & Row, Publishers, Inc., 49 East
33rd Street, New York, N.Y. 10016. Published simultaneously in Canada by
Fitzhenry & Whiteside Limited, Toronto.*

LIBRARY OF CONGRESS CATALOG CARD NUMBER: 70-148435

*This book is lovingly
dedicated to
my Parents*

CONTENTS

Illustrations follow pages 52 and 116

INVITATION TO JOY

CHAPTER ONE

Prelude to New Joy

PARIS. October 5, 1956. It was my birthday. My husband and I were staying at the Ritz in a lovely suite overlooking the hotel's interior garden. We had just finished lunching with our friend Art Buchwald, who was then the *New York Herald Tribune*'s Paris columnist. Art had come to interview my husband as the first American stable owner to fly horses from the United States to France specifically for the Prix de l'Arc de Triomphe, Europe's richest horse race. We were running two fine thoroughbreds, Fisherman and Career Boy, and had brought two of America's most famous jockeys, Sam Boulmetis and Eddie Arcaro, to ride them. We had also flown over our trainers and more than a week's supply of food and water for the horses. After all, even in Paris horses can't drink wine.

I enjoyed the horse talk but I loved Paris more. After luncheon I excused myself from the gentlemen and took a leisurely stroll down the Rue St. Honoré. It was one of those glowing autumn days when the sky is crystal clear and the chestnut trees lining the streets are just beginning to turn to a warm gold. The excitement of the coming race, the beautiful weather, and the fact that it was my birthday combined to make that October day a special one. I made some purchases in the delightful specialty shops that sell handbags,

gloves, and perfumes, and then paused at other windows to
consider what additional trinket could give me a moment
of pleasure. I was wearing a new outfit, a birthday gift from
my husband. It was a two-piece dress with a wraparound skirt
and a coat to match. They were made of baize wool material
in pale Eton blue with the seams outlined by bands of nut-
brown suede. Eton blue and brown were the colors of our
racing silks.

Tired of shopping, I went along the Rue Royale across the
Place de la Concorde and to the Tuileries Garden, where I
rested before returning to the Ritz to dress for my birthday
party, which was to be held at the Lido, a famous cabaret
restaurant on the Champs Elysées . . .

That day in Paris has now become symbolic of my life as
Mrs. Cornelius Vanderbilt Whitney. Life was busy and interesting with endless variety and opportunity. My marriage had
brought me all the worldly possessions one could think of.
To most everybody, including myself, it seemed a full and
satisfying existence. I lived the kind of life that many people
refer to as "the abundant life." In a certain sense my life was
abundant, but since that afternoon on the Rue St. Honoré
I have discovered that the word "abundant" has a much
deeper meaning than that reflected by my life as Mrs. C. V.
Whitney. I cannot deny that during my sixteen years of marriage my life was full of pleasures. But those pleasures were
on the surface; they had no cohesion, no depth, no sure
foundation. It was not until I had an inner awakening and
God gave my life a new dimension that I experienced genuine
and abundant joy. In outward appearances I did not change
radically. The change was an inner one, a change of the heart.
Within a year after that October afternoon in Paris I would
come to discover that there are two kinds of abundance: that
which appears to be full, satisfying, and abiding, and that
which really is radiant and joyful.

The year 1956 was the prelude to my awakening to new joy. It was a typical year in my married life, as full of dazzling entertainment and material riches as anyone could hope for. But behind its façade hid an emptiness and a purposelessness that glitter and glamor and being on-the-go could not disguise.

Deserts and Canyons

Early in 1956 my husband, Cornelius Vanderbilt Whitney, always called Sonny, and I were in Scottsdale, Arizona, staying at Camelback Inn. One of my great pleasures in being out West is that it is Indian country. I had visited the Sioux Indians in South Dakota with my mother and father when I was younger and have had a lifelong interest in Indian peoples and culture.

During our marriage Sonny and I had visited many tribes. We had ridden to the Papago village near Tucson where floodwater farming, perfected in the first century A.D., is still practiced. We had also become acquainted with the proud, brave Taos Indians who at long last have been granted the land around Blue Lake, the mountain pool out of which, according to legend, their primal ancestors rose. On another trip we had packed into Havasu Canyon, a western spur of Grand Canyon, to spend several days with the little-known Havasupai, the "people of the blue-green water." To reach their territory we descended almost straight down from the canyon rim through corridors of towering stone. Suddenly, in a barren stony gorge we came upon a great pool, dyed brilliant aquamarine by the high limestone content of the springs that feed it. From it runs a creek which divides into three waterfalls—two higher than Niagara—that plunge to the floor of the canyon. The Havasupai breed sturdy pack ponies and raise vegetables and fruit, especially peaches, in their isolated tropical paradise.

But the Indian tribe we know most intimately is the
Hopi of eastern Arizona. Early in the 1950s Sonny and I
became close friends of Chief Porter Timeche and visited in
his home with our son Searle and my stepdaughter Gail.
While we were in Arizona in the winter of 1956 I was able
to persuade him to bring members of his tribe to Camelback
Inn for an exhibition of dances and crafts.

We had first seen the Hopi ceremonial dances when as
guests of Chief Porter at Shongopavi on the Second Mesa we
attended the kachina dances which are held in the sacred
kiva, or underground council chamber. The kiva was built
in the side of a cliff and the men entered it by means of a
ladder from the ground level. In the late afternoon they
congregated there to conduct tribal business, smoke a peace
pipe, share a meal, and prepare for the dances. It was not
until almost midnight that the women, children, and guests
were allowed to enter—not down the men's ladder but
through a small opening in the side of the mesa wall. We
shivered on the high, narrow ledge under bright stars while
waiting for the door to be opened from the inside; the barren
desert, stretching for miles in the distance, was bathed in
eerie moonlight. Our bodies pulsated with the vibrations of
the tomtoms beating under the ground.

Finally we were let into the dimly lighted kiva and were
guided to little wooden benches along the edge of the chamber. Then the dances began. The men had completely painted
their bodies with bright pigments made from pulverized desert rock and colored sand. Their carved cottonwood masks
were adorned with billowing feathers, and fox and other
animal skins hung swinging over their buttocks. Pine boughs
transported many miles from the mountains were wound
around their waists. Electric blue turquoise bracelets and
wampum decorated their wrists and chests. Behind their
knees some dancers wore turtle shells filled with stones, and
around their waists were belts made from the hooves of small

animals. These added a dry rattling rhythm to the deep resonance of the drums and the scratchy beat of the hand gourds. Kachina dances are accompanied by quarter-tone chantings; they tell religious and mythical stories and are often dramatized prayers. The dancers, who in everyday life are fathers, husbands, farmers, and artisans, become incarnations of the tribal gods and legendary heroes.

The performance of Chief Porter Timeche and his Hopis given at Camelback was spectacular and very enthusiastically received by the guests at the Inn. Their exhibition and sale of water-color paintings, silver jewelry, woven baskets, and woolen fabrics made into shawls, belts, and skirts was also successful. It was my hope that the display would stimulate a greater appreciation of the high artistic achievement of which the Indians are so justly proud and a greater sympathy toward their plight as dispossessed Americans.

That winter in Arizona we also spent a good deal of time in the brilliantly colored Monument Valley where Sonny's film production company was shooting *The Searchers*. Sonny had organized the company with his World War II buddy, Merian C. Cooper, the producer of *King Kong*. They hoped to develop an "American Series" which would depict with historical accuracy the dramatic growth of our country. Patriotism, man's struggle with nature, and the opening of the West were to be central themes, and the Indians were to be treated fairly for a change. The first of the only two movies completed and released was *The Searchers*, directed by John Ford and starring John Wayne and Natalie Wood.

I'll never forget my arrival on location. No sooner had we sat down for our first dinner than a dreadful fight broke out among the crew. Crockery flew, tables and benches overturned, men punched, tackled, rolled, and shouted. I was horrified! Then abruptly the fracas stopped as suddenly as it had begun. The men cheered and laughed. The fight had been an exhibition staged by John Ford and put on by the stunt men as a welcome to me. Later John Ford gave me a very short walk-on part as a hymn-singing graveside mourner. This was my introduction to film making.

The Searchers was filmed on a Navajo reservation, and many tribesmen were employed as extras or in the crew. They generously made Sonny and me honorary members of the tribe.

Royal Wedding

While we were making *The Searchers* I joined Sonny for a short trip to Los Angeles. While he was attending to business I visited the Hollywood studios of Metro-Goldwyn-Mayer to watch our friend, Grace Kelly, who was filming *The Philadelphia Story*. From the dazzling California sunshine I entered the vast, pitch-dark shed in which lighted movie sets sparkled like jewels on black velvet. I passed a storefront, a hospital solarium, a business office, and a corner of a formal garden—all looking complete, but in reality only shallow façades. How like our own lives at times; from the outside they look strong and whole, but inside there is emptiness— nothing at all.

Grace was in the midst of filming a scene on a sun porch. My visit was a surprise, but she is as untemperamental as she is beautiful and during a break she greeted me with real warmth. She took me to her trailer dressing room and showed me photographs of handsome Prince Rainier of Monaco. Their engagement had just been announced, and she told me about their plans with delightful gaiety and simplicity. The wedding was to be in Monaco in April, and she invited Sonny and me to come.

As the world knows, the wedding was televised, reported, and photographed for all the newspapers and magazines. To be there was like being in fairyland. Monaco with its castle, its cathedral, and its casino climbs steeply up the cornice to the north and overlooks the sparkling blue Mediterranean to the south. That April the Riviera was bursting with spring flowers, azure skies, and decorated streets, shops, and houses as native Monagasques, friends, and dignitaries from the world over came together to witness the magnificent ceremony.

I watched the small civil ceremony on television in the lobby of the Hotel Hermitage with Randolph Churchill and other friends on April 18, and the next day attended the wedding ceremony at the Cathedral of St. Nicholas. Great baskets overflowing with lilies and white lilacs and entwined with ribbons in the colors of the United States and Monaco had been hung from the chandeliers. Nadia Boulanger conducted the chorus and orchestra and a fanfare of silver trumpets announced the arrival of the bride. Grace is one of the most completely beautiful women I have ever known and I have never seen anyone more elegant than she was in her wedding gown of ivory bisque peau de soie with a lace bodice and a long train. Her lace veil was attached to a close-fitting coif, similar to those seen in sixteenth-century paintings. Prince Rainier was in full-dress uniform with rows of medals and the royal Monagasque ribbon across his chest. After the ceremony, which lasted for two hours and was in French and in English, the Prince and Princess went briefly to another church for special prayers while the wedding guests walked up the winding hill to the palace courtyard and gardens for the reception.

My outfit, designed by Mr. John, was a two-piece gown of rosy pink chiffon with a low back draping. With it I wore pink chiffon gloves and a matching wide-brimmed hat with darker rose velvet underbrimming. I also wore a strand of large pinkish pearls, lustrous and perfectly matched, once owned by the Empress Eugénie of France. I remember wearing them when we were in Spain and visited the Duke of Alba. The Duke, who was a nephew of the Empress, told me that he used to play with those very pearls when, as a child, he sat on his aunt's lap. I was strangely moved when he asked me if he could touch them once again in remembrance of that great lady.

There were various parties before and after the wedding. One I enjoyed particularly was given by Aristotle Socrates Onassis aboard his yacht *Christina*. The ship is really a floating mansion. Among the many paintings, a most beautiful El Greco Madonna hangs over the library desk. Under the glass top of the bar tiny model boats depicting the history of ships from the Ark, a Roman galley, a Mississippi steamboat to a Greek óil tanker float in procession drawn by magnets over a green glass sea. Marble and lapis lazuli are used for the fireplaces, doorknobs, and stair rails. Ari is a perfect host, with a great sense of humor and an infectious laugh.

The only cloud in those wedding skies was my disappointment that Sonny had not been able to be with me. He had urged me to go alone, although I had never accepted an invitation without him before and I missed him.

Celebration at Old Westbury

When I returned from Monaco, I was immediately immersed in preparing for a great double party to be held at Whitney House in June to celebrate Sonny's and my fifteenth wedding anniversary and also to present to society his seventeen-year-old daughter Gail.

I had decided to convert the indoor tennis court into a carnival scene. During the winter the groundsmen on the estate had cut from our woods four large maple trees; they were now painted white and placed, one in each corner of the court area. I wanted them without leaves so they could be hung with big red and white paper balls. Hundreds of balls were also suspended from the tennis court ceiling, completely obliterating its glass panes. Paintings of harlequins covered the entire surface of the backboard walls, and to carry out the motif, I designed special wrought-iron chairs—the circus colors of their round cushions made it seem as if a bale of bright confetti had been spilled into the room. The table-cloths were white and were appliqued with very large colored diamond-shaped felt.

Our carpenters built two stairways leading down from the balcony overlooking the court. Between them they con-structed a special platform for Lester Lanin's orchestra, over which hung a red-and-white-striped canopy. They also laid a wooden dance floor over the entire court area.

To complete the carnival theme—or rather to start it off from our guests' point of view—we engaged jugglers and acro-bats to perform in an open-sided tent by the entrance. Thus, as our friends drew up in their cars, they were introduced to the carnival mood of the evening.

Two hundred and fifty of our close friends were invited to dine with us. We had Hungarian and light concert music during dinner, with dancing between courses. Sonny's sister Barbara, now Mrs. George Headley, gave a dinner for Gail and fifty of her friends at the Grecian Studio on the estate. About midnight, five hundred more guests joined us for the dance honoring Gail's debut. We danced all night—until seven the next morning—to Lester Lanin's music, alternating with a rock and roll band.

It was a cold night for June, but we had a roaring fire in the drawing room of the tennis house and we warmed and cheered ourselves before it when we were not dancing. It was an enchanting evening.

Parisian Veneer

Memories of the past year flooded my mind as I sat in the Tuileries Garden on that crisp October afternoon. The past year had been a full and exciting one, but despite all that

I had seen and experienced there remained a void at the very core of me. I wondered if I were asking too much of life. Later I would realize I had been asking too little. I watched the children guiding their drifting boats in the boat basin. I sensed that I was drifting too—drifting from party to party, shop to shop, country to country. There was no direction, no goal, and seemingly no guiding hand in my life.

I shook myself from my reverie and dashed back to the hotel to dress for the party that evening. The Lido was fun and gay, but served only to add another layer of shiny veneer over my growing restlessness.

Another layer was added two days later when the Prix de l'Arc de Triomphe race at Longchamps track was run. In spite of the crisp weather, the crowd on October 7, the day of the race, was one of the most elegant I have ever seen. Fur bonnets were in vogue that season, and the intermittent rain collected in glistening drops on the pelts of mink, seal, fox, and sable. The Longchamps track is among the most picturesque in the world. The track is turf, a sort of egg-shaped oval, hilly, and quite long by American standards. It uses white webbing rather than gates at the starting line, and red balls on standards mark the finish. The Arc de Triomphe race is begun to the far right of the grandstands, opposite the ancient windmill of the Abbey of Notre Dame de l'Humilité. The horses run in a clockwise direction, backwards for us. Fisherman, ridden by Sam Boulmetis, kept the lead for the first mile and a quarter, back of a group of trees, up a hill and down, until the turn for the home stretch. Then an Italian entry, Ribot, came to the head and won. Career Boy didn't like the hills at all and lost himself on them, but when he reached the flat he wanted to run forever, and actually came in fourth by a nostril.

Our dear friend Prince Aly Khan gave a small dinner for us at Maxim's. I sat between him and his eighty-year-old father, His Highness the Aga Khan. In my travel book this well-known citizen of the world wrote:

> Life is a great noble destiny
> Not a mean and groveling thing to
> be shuffled through as best we can,
> but a lofty, noble calling.

A few days later, as a parting gesture, he and his majestic wife, the Begum, sent me the most stunning arrangement of flowers I have ever beheld. There were two and a half dozen pink roses and one and a half dozen pink tiger lilies, stephanotis, and a very large bunch of lilies of the valley, centered with a spray of twelve white butterfly orchids. Tucked in the front left corner were two magnificent purple orchids with magenta throats. The words the Aga Khan wrote, and his and the Begum's thoughtfulness in sending the beautiful floral creation, somehow symbolize for me the high purpose, the beauty and joy, by which our lives can be governed. I had not yet done so, but in the years that followed, I found my life's "lofty, noble calling": it is to praise God and to share his transforming love.

CHAPTER TWO

Buckeye Girl with a Song

PLYMOUTH, Ohio, is one of those salt-of-the-earth towns in the heartland of America. It is peaceful, with a jagged pentagon-shaped "square" as its center and streets lined with towering, gracefully arching elm trees, making of the roadways delightful tunnels of verdant light and shadow.

In the early 1900s my family built their three-story home on the southwestern side of the square. I was born in the front upstairs bedroom, a room with a large bay window which commanded a view of the square and of the school and church. The house had a long, wide porch stretching across its front. How I loved swinging high over the driveway in the great brown-stained oak porch swing, balancing it carefully so that it would not break the window next to which it was perilously hung. Around the side of the house, through a white arched gate, was a garden walk leading to the "three-hole outdoor library." That was a place of shivering in the winter, but in summer the walk was bordered by myriads of flowers and it was lovely to skip through the garden. Until I was in grade school, our family, like most others in town, managed without running water or indoor plumbing. We didn't have electricity either, but I remember the soft light of the gas flame shining through the cut-glass shades of the chandeliers and realize that though it may have lacked modern conveniences, our home was brimming with warmth and comfort.

Plymouth stands in a "salad bowl," halfway between Cleveland and Columbus, equidistant between Sandusky, Norwalk, and Mansfield, right on the Richland and Huron county line —our house is in Richland County, and the school across the street is in Huron County. The region is wonderfully fertile, the high limestone content in the water and soil giving the fruit, vegetables, and grains strength which seems to bolster wills as well as bodies. I think the goodness of the earth may be a reason so many Buckeyes live to an advanced age, and why the state has produced so many great Americans. Thomas A. Edison, the Wright Brothers, astronaut John Glenn, and six presidents of the United States are among them. Ohio natives are called Buckeyes after the horse chestnut trees' large, round mahogany brown seeds which look just like the velvety eyes of a deer. These tall sturdy trees grow throughout the state and in the springtime have ten- to fifteen-inch-high Christmas-tree-shaped clusters of creamy pale pink blossoms at the tip of each branch.

Plymouth when I was growing up had a population of around two thousand people, and it is about the same today. The Baltimore & Ohio Railroad and the Akron, Canton & Youngstown Railroad go through the town, but it is primarily a farm and livestock center. There was only one industry, the Fate-Root-Heath Co. which made narrow-gauge locomotives and other machinery. Although the farmers and merchants tended to come from long-established families, I remember little discrimination against the people whose work caused them to be more transient. Nor was there antagonism toward the immigrants who arrived from Holland, Hungary, and Rumania to labor on the rich black peat muckland, growing the prime celery and vegetables for which the area is so famous. They didn't speak much English, were poor, kept to their old-world traditions, and were generally Roman Catholic whereas the older settlers were Protestant, but I cannot recall any antiforeign or antireligious sentiment in home, school, or church. There were a few Jewish families, too, but I was unaware that their religion was different from mine. Since there was no synagogue, many of them came to our Lutheran Church for social activities and sometimes for worship and Sunday school. Most of the young people left town after high school, but enough have returned, or new families come, to maintain the feeling of a warm and caring community. Plymouth has sheltered and supported me throughout my whole life, and I am grateful for the values and attitudes it taught me. They have given me a sure foundation on which I could rely both in times of trouble and in times of grace. I still love to go home.

In most respects I think I had a typical small-town-America upbringing. I learned to swim in the muddy Huron River, with its plentiful supply of bloodsuckers, then graduated to the icy, ninety-foot-deep water-filled stone quarry. I fed the chickens, gathered the eggs, climbed the railroad trestle, and roller skated daily to the other end of town to get a tin pail filled with fresh warm milk from one of my mother's girlhood friends. It never occurred to any of us to fret about the straw floating in the cream or the little brown particles in the bottom of the bucket. I suppose we were immunized with our own native germs. Miss Briggs, a local milliner, let me come to her shop and try on hats and play with bits of flowers. The Hanick sisters' millinery shop was a few doors away and they, too, showed me their boxes of ribbons and plumes and allowed me to amuse myself with "grown up" hats.

In other ways, though, I think my growing up was special. Perhaps everyone feels this way, but my parents, my preoccupation with medicine and music, and my life in Florida gave me interests not common to every Midwestern schoolgirl.

My father, George James Searle, was an Englishman with

a Boston accent. My mother, Bertha Ann Fenner, was from an old Buckeye family whose ancestors first pushed into upper Ohio by covered wagon during the 1830s. I am proud of both sides of my heritage—sturdy pioneer stock mixed with the ingenuity and incentive of a naturalized American. I was raised to be proud of the constant blending of backgrounds in the United States and proud of Ohio's part in our nation's history.

Born in London during the reign of Queen Victoria, whom he often saw as a lad, my father came to Massachusetts when he was a young boy, with his mother and his stepfather—his father had been killed in an accident—and his half brothers, James and William Miles. More than anything else, he wanted an education. But he was twenty one years old when he was at last able to enter the seventh grade of Nichols Academy, now Nichols College, in Dudley, Massachusetts. And he shoveled snow, cleaned lamps, and tended the library fire for the princely sum of $2.50 a week for his tuition. He graduated in three years, and then worked his way through Boston University School of Medicine.

Following graduation he married Adora Fenner, a Plymouth girl whom he had met while she was studying at the Boston Academy of Music. They settled in Marlboro, Massachusetts, where he began his long career as an eye, ear, nose, and throat specialist and general practitioner. They had three sons, my half brothers Fred and George, Jr., and a baby who, with his mother, died of pneumonia shortly after his birth. My own first awareness of death came when as a child I was told that the mother was buried with her son nestled in her arms.

Grief-stricken, my father took his two boys to their grandparents in Plymouth, Ohio, and then headed west to live with his half brother William, who had homesteaded in a remote area near the northern border of South Dakota. Like other early settlers, they lived in a sod house built into the side of a hill and cooked their food over dry cow dung. While driving cattle from Texas to South Dakota, my father became interested in the many Indian tribes that then ranged the American wilderness. They called him "Sawbones" and came to him when they needed special doctoring. My father respected their traditions, recognizing in their natural remedies many of the ingredients of modern medicines. My father and his brother planted crops. The first year they suffered from wind, then grasshoppers, and then drought. One year, after the cattle drive, my father said, "Well, this is our last chance." And so it was that the homestead on Thunder Butte Creek bore the name Chance. Until recently that was the post office address of the little settlement there; a few years ago the name was changed to Meadow.

My father was a doctor, not a rancher, so before long he returned to Plymouth. There he came to know and love Bertha Ann Fenner, a cousin of his first wife. They married and decided to stay in Plymouth. I was their only child, born to them after they had been married for many years.

My father was a true country doctor in the most hallowed and dedicated sense, providing every kind of medical care, for there was no hospital in the area when he hung out his shingle. He served a region of twenty- to thirty-mile radius for years, first using a horse and buggy and then a Model-T Ford. When the snow was too deep for the buggy, he would unharness the horse and ride bareback through drifts up to the horse's belly to care for his patients. Sometimes he had to chop firewood and melt snow to sterilize his instruments. He was justly proud of his record of bringing over thirteen hundred babies into the world without ever losing a mother.

My father kept office hours twenty-four hours a day. But Saturday was the busiest, for that was the day that the farmers from miles around brought their produce into Plymouth to sell and did their weekly shopping and exchanged gossip and information. All day long, but particularly in the evening, my father's waiting room and our long front porch were crowded with patients who had come to have their aches and pains and sores cared for, their eyes examined, and often just to ask for good advice. My father understood that sometimes a good listening ear was as effective a cure as a pill or a salve. There was one drugstore in town, but it sold mainly patent medicines, and so my father compounded his own prescriptions by grinding herbs and mixing them with oils and essences and medicine. I was intrigued watching him make up the ointments. First he weighed the ingredients carefully on a delicate little brass balance scale. He worked them to a paste on a marble or thick glass slab, moving his spatula surely and rhythmically—making beautiful patterns in the salve as he blended it. Then he lifted the finished unguent all at once on the spatula and slipped it into a little round tin box. I also remember the fine precision with which he wound bandages around a patient's wrist, ankle, leg, or head. I have saved some of Dad's mortars and pestles as a reminder of his creative devotion to medicine and of the grace, beauty, and success with which he healed his patients.

Dad also served the community as mayor, and he was the first health officer of Richland County.

To me, my mother was the loveliest-looking lady in Plymouth. She had warm soft brown eyes as velvety as those of a doe or of a Buckeye. Her long, nearly black hair was piled high on her head, and she always had time to read to me, help me with my studies or listen to me practice for the school play, or make a costume. At the same time, since receptionists and nurses were unheard of in a small-town doctor's office in those days, it was she who calmed the patients when Dad was out on calls and provided twenty-four-hour answering service by telephone and doorbell. She also scrubbed my father's instruments and the equipment in the treatment room, and she washed the office linen in a hand-cranked washing machine, first carrying the rainwater from the cistern and soaking the blood out of the towels. She was a slender woman, but she must have had muscles and a constitution of steel. Today, as I look back, I marvel at her steadfastness. For after an ordeal in the treatment room my father would win the praise and gratitude of the patient, I could run off to my school friends, but Mother was left to mop up. After she finished, she returned patiently and quietly and, most often alone, to the chores of her own housework.

My mother came from strong hardworking stock. Her grandfather Felix Fenner and his wife came from Bethlehem, Pennsylvania, by covered wagon in the early years of the nineteenth century to settle on the rich, rolling farmland of northern Ohio. He prospered. Mother grew up in a large gingerbread-trimmed Victorian house which her father had built on the old homestead. My grandmother was still alive when I was a little girl, and I used to visit her often. From her collection of pioneer kitchenware, the butter churns and bread-kneading troughs brought West by her own mother, I inherited my love of early Americana. Her wonderful attic was full of trunks of costumes and treasures. And I shall never forget the delight of bathing in her enormous tin tub. Three steep steps led up to its rim, cold water filled it from rainwater tanks hidden under the roof beams, and steaming hot water was added by hand.

My maternal great-grandfather was an accomplished musician and came from a devout Lutheran family. A great-uncle, the Rev. Harlan K. Fenner, founded Fenner Memorial Church in Louisville, Kentucky; another Fenner was the first pastor of the English Lutheran Church in Mansfield, Ohio. My great-grandfather and his brother-in-law Samuel Trauger started our Lutheran Church in Plymouth by loaning the money for the building. When the church was unable to repay the loan, these two men stood before the congregation, placed the note on a silver salver, and burned it, saying,

"The note is now satisfied and the loan is paid in full." The parsonage was between our house and the church. It has now been razed and our house is the parsonage.

That church played an important role in my early life. Although my father was an Anglican by birth, he went with my mother and me to the Lutheran Church for worship and socials when his medical practice permitted. For me Sunday school, weekly worship, the Luther League, and choir were a part of everyday life, and I took them very much for granted. My mother was deeply, quietly religious. She was patient, comforting, and extremely generous, always taking baskets of food to friends and patients and helping in thousands of thoughtful ways.

Medical Apprentice

I adored my mother and hope I was a helpful and obedient daughter. But I idolized Daddy, with his piercing steel-blue eyes and his wiry, fast-moving graceful manner which never wasted a motion. I dreamed of following in his medical footsteps. As early as I can remember, I wanted to become a surgeon—not a nurse or even a general practitioner. There were many reasons for this. One was the amount of time I spent with my father. When I was very small, I merely went with Daddy to give him company on his rounds, but by the time I was eight, I actively helped him. In those days minor surgery was often performed on a dining-room or kitchen table in the patient's home. There was no adequate lighting, only what Daddy's head reflector could pick up from an oil lamp or, later, a single electric bulb which tended to make his head cast a shadow on the patient. Sometimes he used a battery-operated head lamp. During a tonsillectomy, I would hold the anesthesia mask in place, keep the ether dropping, and check the patient's state of consciousness by taking the pulse and looking at the eyes. I sponged and handed Daddy the instruments. At that time tonsils were snipped out with a wire snare. After the tonsils and adenoids had been removed, I tipped the patient so the blood would run out into a bucket, turned him back up on the table again, waited for the anesthetic to wear off, and tucked him to bed. Then we went off to see the next patient.

Once I helped Daddy and a surgeon from Mansfield perform an appendectomy in a home. I am happy to say the patient is still living. It was the first time I had looked into the abdominal cavity. Daddy commented on the wonder of God's design of the human body, and I was fascinated by the stomach and the yards of intestine which so ingeniously absorb the food and give us nourishment and earthly life. Later I learned more about the structural beauty of man's body when I helped my father perform autopsies.

Often in the office I gave first aid until Dad came. Many serious injuries occurred on the farms and in the foundry. He cleaned the wounds, stopped the blood, sewed them up, and when necessary, amputated fingers and legs. Since farmers and factory men work with their hands, Dad made a special effort to see that a finger amputation did not destroy the usefulness of the whole hand. He carefully designed skin flaps, covering the ends of the amputated digits so that the stubs would remain flexible. Once Dad grafted a piece of sponge on the end of a patient's shortened thumb and covered it with skin to give the man a soft base for turning nuts and bolts, a task on which his job depended.

Working with my father I learned precision, artistry, care, dedication, and, because we could do only what was humanly possible, trust in the healing powers of God. I was so young when these attitudes toward work and assistance to others were instilled in me that they have been a part of my subconscious approach to the demands of life ever since.

Certainly I was not unique in sharing the responsibilities of my elders. All of my friends in Plymouth helped their parents in their work—be it behind the soda fountain, in the stores, or on the farm. My work was special simply because my father was a doctor and was dealing in matters that concerned life and death. The responsibility involved in my helping him was heightened—though perhaps I was not aware of it at the time—because the work I was asked to perform required ultimate attention, care, and commitment. As a child my primary joy was to work at the side of my father; as an adult I realize that the primary benefit to me was derived from the very seriousness of the work I was asked to perform.

In addition, I had an even more personal reason for my interest in medicine, a functional heart condition that has been with me all my life. When I was little I was terrified when my heart palpitated rapidly and produced severe choking pains. Daddy explained that these attacks were triggered by overexcitement or by getting too hot through strenuous play or exercise. And he showed me how to slow down my heartbeat by holding my breath and pressing my ribs firmly with a tightened diaphragm and air-filled lungs, exerting force on my heart to hold it still until everything went black and the beat became normal again. Happily, I knew enough about the body to realize you cannot hold your breath until you die, for when you pass out, you inhale again. The therapy is nevertheless frightening. Just before the regular beat begins I experience a sensation which is like hot black molasses pouring over my head, running slowly past my eyes and blinding me. Then my heart seems to give a final squeeze, increasing the pain in my throat, the palpitation stops and my heart resumes its regular steady beat.

When I was an adult I was given a scientific diagnosis of my heart condition. The palpitations are auricular paroxysmal tachycardia caused by insufficient vagal inhibition of the heart. Because of my interest in cardiovascular medicine I recently watched Dr. Michael DeBakey, the famed Houston

surgeon, perform four open heart operations, and as I saw
him and his staff remove a vein from a thigh and attach it to
the heart while the blood was circulated by a heart-lung
machine, I remembered that my father had made predictions
about surgical advances and the possibility of transplanting
parts of the body. For Dad was not only a country doctor,
par excellence, he was also enthusiastic about scientific medical progress. Nearly every night till midnight he was at his
desk, studying large medical tomes, and he usually went to
New York or Philadelphia in the summertime for postgradu-
ate training and to keep up with latest research. He had great
inventiveness, and made copious notes of his surgical operations long before others discovered the same procedures and
put them in medical books.

I must have inherited my father's scientific interest, for
except for the courses in biology and physiology, I received
only average grades in high school. One principal said I
should never get "A's" because I would not apply myself.
But when it came to cutting up earthworms and frogs or
studying the human body, extra effort was no problem at all.
In fact, I was in my academic element when it came to tracing
the path of food as it travels from the mouth through the
body and turns into skin, fingernails, or the iris of the eye.
The reason I was not more interested in ancient history and
algebra may have been that the school building was practically in our garden and I was constantly reminded of the
more fascinating things I could be doing with my father if
only I were at home.

In spite of my heart condition I was basically healthy as a
child. I had only one acute illness, a severe enteritis and
colitis, or intestinal infection, when I was eight or nine years
old. The ailment was traced to tainted drinking water when
a dead rat was found in the school's system. I had to stay
in bed for a month, and the abdominal pain was horrible.
With gentle massage Daddy could relieve my agony only for

short periods. When I grew older my parents told me they hadn't expected me to live.

But like so many painful experiences, this illness had a positive result. Once the infection subsided I was extremely weak and my parents decided I should start calisthenics to build strength; unknowingly I was instilled with the importance of exercise in a healthy life. I did pushups and backbends, high kicks, and muscle flexing. Often Dad called me to demonstrate my skill to patients who needed exercise therapy. "Here is 'Nuisance,'" he would say, introducing me by his pet name—I was always tagging after him, asking him endless questions—"and she will show you how to get that leg working again and the kinks out of that back." I can still bend forward and put the palms of my hands flat on the floor from an upright position. Neither when I was eight nor now do I see exercise as a rigid program. But it can be carried on in everyday activities and it is fun. For instance, when you want something from the floor you should stoop with straight back so leg muscles are used; when you reach you should really reach. When writing letters, or telephoning, or signing checks, your ankles and shoulders and fingers can rotate, and your abdominal muscles flex. You can trot or run for a taxi. And it is always possible to practice deep breathing, to hold in the tummy, keep the back straight and chin in—it is a good idea to train yourself to do two or three things at once. In this way you can accomplish a routine of exercises by the end of a normal day's work. Often I practice singing scales and vocal exercises and rotate my shoulders, hands, and ankles while working at my desk or waiting at stop lights when driving my car.

Oranges and Alligators

Before I was in grade school, a rather unusual—for Plymouth, Ohio—pattern imposed itself on our home life. My older half brother Fred, who had been an agronomist but was fighting in France during World War I, died of pneumonia. He left part of his Florida citrus groves and tomato farms to my father. Dad bought out his widow's interest in the property and our family—my mother and father and myself—started the new and happy custom of wintering in Florida.

The first year we drove from Plymouth to Buckingham in a Model-T Ford, and it took thirty days. Breakdowns, muddy roads, and sketchy maps made planning ahead unreliable. Usually we were near no hotel or inn by late afternoon, and we simply camped the night by the side of the road. Forever inventive, Mummy and Daddy had turned the car into their own version of a mobile home. Daddy put hinges on the bottom of the back of the front seat so it could be laid down to meet the level of the back seat, making a bed. The left running board was built up to form a food locker with a lid and a lock. The back seat held a trunk; my doll and I rode in the corner beside it. At night a tarpaulin was attached to one side of the car in order to make a lean-to under which one of us slept. While Mummy cooked over a campfire, Daddy spent hours every evening vulcanizing sure-to-be-needed spare inner tubes. In this way we inched south, tires blowing out every few miles, hardly making it up the hills because of our heavy load. Daddy used to ask me to help. "Push, Nuisance," he would order, "push hard on the back seat and help us get up this hill." We slipped and slid across the red clay of south Georgia and at last arrived at our lovely isolated house beside the Orange River in Buckingham, near Fort Myers.

I enjoyed the life of the Orange River country. I used to sit on the roof of the barn and sing at the top of my lungs, watching the lazy alligators sunning along the river. I could see diamondback rattlers as they slithered over the riverbanks and through the sand under the orange trees. Although snakes don't frighten me, I kept a respectful distance. I liked to ride the mules as they pulled the plow or carried baskets full of ripe tomatoes from the fields. I carried a salt shaker and ate those hot, luscious fruits all day, never caring if I swallowed more juice or mule sweat.

When I was school age I transferred early each winter to a one-room Florida country school. The Florida children did not understand my "Yankee" accent and I did not understand their Southern drawl—perhaps it was a good experience in linguistic guesswork! In the spring I went back to Plymouth to complete the year with my class there.

Daddy made a valiant attempt to turn a profit on the citrus and tomatoes. But after we had been to Buckingham for three or four winters, he realized he was no grove man and sold the property. Since he had become a bona-fide Florida booster, he couldn't think of leaving the state and bought a new winter home in Bradenton, near Sarasota and forty-two miles south of Tampa.

Our home in Bradenton had a large camellia garden shaded by a slat trellis. Mummy, who was called "Miss Ann" by her Florida neighbors, held "court" on the sun porch overlooking the wide Manatee River or on her upstairs balcony. Daddy loved the fishing and gardening. Not owning groves did not prevent him from experimenting with papayas, encouraging the landowners to develop larger potatoes or to plant soybeans in order to diversify their orange-grapefruit-gladioli-dependent economy.

When I entered high school, splitting my education between Florida-Ohio was impossible. But by then my half brother George was a licensed physician. He took over Dad's Plymouth practice each winter, and I stayed north with him and the housekeeper. George was tall, brown-eyed, and serious-minded. Since he was doing graduate work as well as taking care of Dad's patients, he was always very busy, but nevertheless he was generous and loving and fun to be with.

Florida remained our second home, and as the years went by, my parents extended their visits there.

As I look back, my childhood and adolescence were extraordinarily happy. I had time for everything—for helping Dad and planning to be a surgeon, for studying, for heading the debating society, for being the basketball team's cheerleader, for church worship and work, for picking bouquets of violets, trillium, and jack-in-the-pulpits in the meadows, for summer walks to the "mud hole" swimming spot on the Huron River, and for studying the offerings of the Sears Roebuck catalogue in the "outdoor library." I also found time, like so many children of my age, for piano lessons with the local music teacher.

Music Everywhere

As a youngster I was surrounded by music. Daddy had a fine, though untrained, tenor voice. I can hear him still, singing Irish love songs, college songs, and the doggie lullabies he had learned as a cowhand driving cattle from Texas to South Dakota to keep the cattle from stampeding or when circling them at night. Mummy played the piano and George, the violin. I started my piano lessons at age ten. I remember Mrs. Shafer, my teacher, always filed her nails during the sessions, but I must have learned something from her. Much more entertaining than lessons was playing and singing together with my family. We also listened to good recorded music— concerts and operas played on a hand-wound Victrola with triangular-cut bamboo needles. I remember putting on the longest recording we had, "Ai Nostri Monti" and "Miserere" from *Il Trovatore* by Verdi, racing to the kitchen and trying to finish the dinner dishes before it ended. We went to Cleveland for live musical performances and for theater. I shall never forget seeing Lady Diana Manners in Max Reinhardt's *The Miracle.*

Outside my family, the two persons who most influenced me musically were "Uncle John" Root, an excellent pianist as well as the president of the Fate-Root-Heath Co., and T. S. Davis, our school superintendent who brought a great variety of musical opportunities to our community. Mother and Dad encouraged me to sing, Mrs. Shafer taught me notes, but "Uncle John" inspired me to want to sing. "Uncle John" accompanied me for my first public solo. I was thirteen and sang "Love Sends a Little Gift of Roses" and "Marcheta" at a social function held at the church. Later, I joined the church choir.

Then Mr. Davis came to town and started a high school chorus, giving me my first introduction to seriously performed choral work. He drilled and trained us as if we were professionals. Because I showed particular interest and aptitude, I was chosen to direct the group in concert. The chorus stood in a semicircle and I, at the right end, indicated the beat and the entrances and cut-offs by a slight but definite nod of my head.

Mr. Davis also prepared our high school chorus to give an operetta each year. Johnny Root, "Uncle John's" son, and I inevitably had the leads. Johnny had the most magnificent untrained tenor voice I have ever heard, and he was my best friend. Our families' properties adjoined, and so we had played together as children. Often we went to the foundry in the afternoons to watch the men "drop the bottom," that is, release the hot molten metal. I was exhilarated by the drama and brilliance of the fiery metal. Maybe it is because they remind me of the smelter in Plymouth that I like to visit mining and smelting operations. I am also fascinated by the fiery spewing of volcanos.

Johnny and I sang many duets in the school productions of such operettas as *Belle of Barcelona* and *In the Garden of the Shah*. If there was a role for a princess, I got it, for although I was a tall, skinny teenager—my friends called me "Shadow"

and "Spindle Shanks" and "Mosquito Legs"—my mother
would create a beautiful costume lavish with beads and lace
and often a pearly crown. Sometimes I was permitted to wear
my grandmother's black lace mantilla. It gives me an odd feeling of continuity—even of completion—to realize that I wore
the same mantilla in 1969 when Archbishop Terence Cooke
of New York was elevated to the College of Cardinals, in
St. Peter's Basilica in Rome.

I practiced my singing in our parlor adjoining Dad's waiting room. Sometimes Daddy opened the door so the patients
could enjoy my trills and high notes, and the captive audience
applauded. Can you imagine that anyone thought it entertaining to hear me practicing songs while waiting to see the
doctor? I think my father rather fondly doted on his only
daughter.

What turned out to be a major event in my musical training came during my sophomore year in high school, for I
met a genuine New York vocal teacher. She was Mme. Caro-
line Lowe who came to Lima, a town not far from Plymouth,
to visit her sister, a friend of Mrs. Shafer, my nail-filing piano
teacher. Mrs. Shafer arranged for me to sing for Mme. Lowe,
who actually was more renowned as an organist than as a
vocal coach. Fortunately, her voice-training techniques were
sound and my voice developed well. I was luckier than some
vocal students I know, for vocal cords are tender and need
very careful nurturing, especially during the teens.

Mme. Lowe thought I had a good voice and potentially a
good musical future. She came to Lima each summer for three
months and gave me a series of lessons. She helped me build a
repertoire of concert pieces and I, of course, was starry-eyed
and determined to go directly to New York after high school
so I could continue to study with the one and only Mme.
Lowe.

My parents, however, said I was too young and must go to
college first. I suggested that I go with them to Florida instead.

They insisted on college, but agreed that I could choose a school there. The only college I knew about near Bradenton was Florida Southern College in Lakeland; it was Methodist and specialized in the liberal arts.

Although pleased to be near my parents in wintertime and quite happy at Florida Southern, my heart was in New York. I'm sure I absorbed a great supply of new knowledge, yet sometimes I think the only thing I learned that did me any good in later years was that a pencil eraser works better on ink if you spit on it!

Loyally committed to Mme. Lowe as a voice teacher, I took no vocal training at college. I studied theory, harmony, counterpoint, history of music, sight reading, piano, and languages. I sang with a sextet and made numerous concert and recital appearances. The year was well spent—even though the dean of women campused me for a week for kissing a boy under a palm tree. It was such an innocent kiss, and right by a street light!

New York, New York

Either I matured greatly in my parents' eyes during my college year or my begging was too much to endure, for, even though I was still in my teens, they gave me permission to study music in New York the following winter. They made elaborate plans for my welfare there. I was to live with Mme. Lowe and her husband, a Columbia University professor, in their apartment at 50 West 67th Street, have a daily voice lesson, practice during the daylight hours, and take evening courses at Columbia in theory, harmony, languages, and other subjects helpful to a musical career.

My expectations were grand. I wanted to be an opera star, for opera combines singing with the drama, movement, and excitement of the theater. I knew the path from Pennsylvania Station to roles in *Tosca* and *Madame Butterfly* was anything but easy, but I was willing to try—to study and practice without fail every day, to sing in choruses and concerts, to audition for Broadway, in short, to do anything that would give me a chance to sing.

Mme. Lowe charged ten dollars a lesson, which was too costly for those days. In addition, I paid her room and board and was expected to tidy the apartment occasionally. Her studio where I had my lessons was in Chickering Hall across from Carnegie Hall on West 57th Street. I practiced in the apartment at least eight hours a day, learning a variety of songs and opera scores. In the evenings I took the subway uptown for the courses at Columbia University.

West 67th Street near Central Park was the heart of the artistic world. Many well-known painters, designers, illustrators, writers, and musicians lived in that short block. I knew several of the artists, and they often asked me to pose for them. I welcomed the extra income and found watching them work extremely interesting. Sometimes they would draw or paint a portrait of me as a present.

Most evenings when I didn't have classes at Columbia I went by myself or with friends to concerts, opera, or the theater. Carnegie Hall was, and I suppose still is, my favorite New York concert hall. Though not the newest auditorium, I think it has the finest acoustics of any in the world. I have always liked to move around in Carnegie Hall, hearing the music from different angles. Often we students would stretch out on the floor at the back of the very top balcony and listen to the music. Even up there we could hear the softest most delicate tones.

At the opera we bought standing-room tickets, and we wandered from level to level so as to hear and see the performances from whatever perspective we chose. Sometimes I feel confined in my box at the new Metropolitan Opera House at Lincoln Center, for I miss being able to view the performance from different perspectives.

In many ways I was not very sophisticated about New York concert life. During my first winter in New York I remember splurging on seats for a performance of *Norma* because Rosa Ponselle was singing. My brother George was coming to New York, and I knew how much he would appreciate hearing that combination of opera and prima donna. The tickets were something like twenty-five dollars each. I did not know it was a benefit, or even what a benefit was. Ponselle was magnificent, but I walked everywhere for weeks because I had bought the tickets with money budgeted for carfare.

That experience, however, gave me an idea for spending my summers in Plymouth profitably: I started the "Eleanor Searle Benefit Concert Series." For the first concert I had dated tickets printed. That seemed uneconomical, because the tickets were handed in at the door and there was nothing to do but throw them away. The next year I ordered undated tickets and used them, year after year. They were sold in all the local stores and by friends. I encouraged patrons to buy five tickets and have their names in the program. My concert hall was the Lutheran Church sanctuary, from which I was allowed to remove the pulpit and altar. I spread Mother's Persian rugs over the chancel steps, banked the front with flowers, and rented a grand piano. I sang such songs as "The Lass with the Delicate Air" by Arne and "My Mother Bids Me Bind My Hair" by Haydn; "Nymphs and Shepherds" by Purcell; the "Waltz Song" from *Romeo and Juliette* by Gounod and the "Ballatella" from *Pagliacci* by Leoncavallo; "Vissi D'arte" from *Tosca* by Puccini, always including a sacred aria from an oratorio or cantata—Bach's "My Heart Ever Faithful," Handel's "Let the Bright Seraphim" or "O Had I Jubal's Lyre," for example. Sometimes Mme. Lowe, also on summer vacation, accompanied me. For a month I would write preconcert publicity for the weekly and daily papers in the area. Then, after the concert, I wrote my own reviews. These were quite some "benefit" concerts. I benefited nicely. It was only after several years that I realized that "benefit performances" were supposed to "benefit" some charitable organization.

One winter when I had been ill, I stayed at home in Plymouth. I had forty-two vocal students every week, directed the church choir, and organized many choral concerts. We sang the Hallelujah Chorus from Handel's *Messiah,* choruses from *The Creation* of Haydn, and Rossini's *Stabat Mater* in which I sang the difficult "Inflamatus" solo. As none of the singers could read music, I taught all parts by rote, many of which we sang in the original Latin. "Uncle John" cooperated in this church and community project by playing the organ.

In spite of the long hours of studying and practicing I did have time for a very pleasant social life in New York. The camaraderie among the music students gave me a sense of belonging although New York even then was thought of as an impersonal city and I was far from home. For instance, when I first came to New York I was "adopted" by the family of Dorothea Ruppe, now Mrs. Sheldon Baker, another of Mme. Lowe's students. Dotty's father was a doctor and his office was attached to their apartment. I felt very much at home there, and I used to run with their two huge red Chow dogs in Riverside Park. I also liked the wonderful parties they had almost every Saturday evening, which many young people attended.

Friends sometimes visited me from Ohio—although the trip to New York was a once-in-a-lifetime excursion to most Buckeyes. Joe Sittler, who helped me move the pulpit and arrange the church for my benefit concerts, came to New York several times. He was then a student at Wittenberg College in Springfield, Ohio, and is now one of America's most eminent theologians. In those days, though, we just had fun riding the double-decker buses down Fifth Avenue, poking around the pushcarts on the lower East Side and dining in Chinatown. Although double-decker buses have vanished

from Fifth Avenue, Dr. Joseph Sittler, Jr. and his wife Jeanne
are still my friends!

Another of my Ohio friends—but he had lived for years
and years in New York—was Daniel Frohman. He and his
brother Charles had had fabled careers with the theater—
they had been producers on Broadway, owned theaters, and as
was the custom in the early 1900s, "owned" famous artists.
When I arrived "Uncle Dan" Frohman was in his eighties
and no longer actively participating in Broadway, but he was
still very much of a presence. He was tall and elegant with a
Van Dyke goatee. He lived in a special apartment on the top
of the Lyceum Theater, and when I dined with him there
we would, if we wanted, watch the play on stage through an
opening in the dining-room panelling. Oftimes we would go
to another theater, so that I must have seen every play on
Broadway. "Uncle Dan" said he went mainly for an after-
dinner sleep—puckishly quipping that from seasoned experience he could easily judge how successful a play was by the
number of times the applause wakened him. He snored too,
which embarrassed me, but everybody knew who he was and
took it for granted as his august right. Whenever I wanted
theater seats to entertain my friends, "Uncle Dan" would arrange for me to have his box in the Lyceum Theater. What
pleasure he brought to my New York life.

The first professional singing jobs I had in New York were
in churches. It still is the very best way for a student to gain
experience as a soloist and at the same time earn extra income. Talk among colleagues at the studio acted as a sort of
perpetual information agency as to what positions were available, so when I heard that the Lutheran Church of the Advent on Broadway at 93rd Street needed a soprano soloist I
applied, and was hired. I sang there for a long time, during
which I came to know the pastor, Dr. Augustus Steimle, and
his family very well. Their daughter Mildred was one of my
closest friends, a son Douglas is a lawyer with the firm which

handled my affairs, and the other son Dr. Edmund Augustus Steimle is professor of homiletics at Union Theological Seminary in New York.

A higher-salaried position lured me to Holy Trinity Episcopal Church, on East 88th Street. There I met Frank Ward, the organist, and a composer in his own right. Mr. Ward was also organist at Temple Israel, a Reform congregation at Broadway and 91st Street. What he told me about the special demands of singing in the Jewish service excited me. I auditioned for the soprano soloist position in the synagogue and was very pleased when I was hired. There was no choir. All the members of the quartet were Protestant, too. I studied Hebrew with the cantor, Joseph Wolfe, whose family was exceedingly kind, frequently inviting me to their home on the Sabbath or for feast days. During the meal, the cantor would patiently explain the moving history of the Jewish people to a Buckeye Lutheran. Through his tutelage, and the kindness of Rabbi and Mrs. William F. Rosenblum, I developed a deep appreciation of the worship and music of the synagogue and the meaning of the Tanach, the Hebrew Scriptures.

Eventually I settled for two week-end jobs, Temple Israel and North Avenue Presbyterian Church in New Rochelle. I sang at both for many years, even continuing after my marriage while my husband was overseas in World War II. Dr. Robert Gayler, an extraordinarily talented musicologist and the director and accompanist on many fine early Victor recordings, directed the choral work in the New Rochelle church. A master musician, his command of the organ seemed to turn it into a symphony orchestra. He gave complete and creative support to the singers. No matter what I sang it seemed as though I were a tennis ball being tossed aloft by a fountain of waters, effortlessly bouncing from tone to tone. He later accepted the deanship of the school of music at Florida Southern College.

Often I sang five services a weekend—Friday night and

Saturday morning at the temple, and at the church Sunday morning service, a vesper service or an oratorio at four, and finally an evening service, youth meeting, or cantata at night. Of course I continued studying music, for practice never stops for a singer, even if one had achieved the highest success. The adage is true that if you miss one day's singing you notice it yourself; if you miss two your coach notices it; and if you miss three your public knows it. A voice is not like other musical instruments. A violin can be stored and with reasonable care it stays in good condition—a twist of the pegs tunes it; the human voice is a living instrument and every moment of its life it must be protected and nurtured. Its perfection is dependent upon the rest of the body. A sleepless night, an emotional upset, a poor diet, or a cold in the head affects its precision. One of the things a singer learns along with recognition of the importance of scales is sacrifice and sustained commitment to his or her career. For me, this training built upon and strengthened the sense of utter dedication to the work at hand that I had learned when assisting my father in his practice and had observed in my brother's devotion to his patients.

After some time I learned from my musician friends that the rent I was paying was extravagant. So when I came back from my summer in Plymouth, I moved to the apartment of a fellow student and his wife on West 69th Street. I lived in what had once been a maid's room.

Because I still felt I should augment the allowance my parents gave me for my music career I decided to look for an evening job to add to my income from church work. One day I was buying music at Schirmer's on East 43rd Street and I noticed a sign for the Arthur Murray Ballroom Dance Studio by their entrance. I have always liked ballroom dancing and had studied ballet and tap dancing in connection with my singing career. I thought perhaps I could get a job with them. I was interviewed and given the opportunity I wanted, with hours from 6:00 P.M. to 10:00 P.M. I was trained in their techniques of teaching dancing, but I have good rhythm and didn't need much instruction. I had spent many hours dancing in the open-air pavilions along the beaches of Lake Erie, which when I was growing up were considered nice places for high school double dates. I can still remember those enormous dance floors with gigantic mirrored spheres circling in the center, sending rainbows of color onto the moving couples and out into the night.

At the Murray studio I was in charge of the reception desk, taking care of bookings and payments and oiling troubled water for upset students. If an instructor were absent, or a pupil dissatisfied, I would then fill in and teach. The studio wanted me to take the day shift, but I had to save that time for my musical career. I did transfer, however, to their new studio on East 46th Street. One of my jobs was to drop the income of the day in the night deposit box in a bank near Grand Central Station. Each night on the way home I bought a quart of milk at a delicatessen. The milk was for the morning; the bottle for protection on the way home. I remember holding it as a club in case I should need it as I passed by rows of dark warehouses and doorways north of the 66th Street subway stop, now opposite Lincoln Center.

When the friends with whom I was living had their second child, I slept on the living-room sofa for a few months. That was hardly satisfactory, so I accepted the invitation of Helen Lewis, a friend from Cleveland, to share her apartment in Tudor City. Helen was secretary to Ted Wyman, the administrative head of Pan American Airways.

The Eternal Road

As was every other young singer in New York, I was constantly on the lookout for concert and musical comedy audition notices. I stood in more lines, walked onto more bare stages, and heard more "thaannk yoouus" yelled from the recesses of musty dark theaters than I care to remember. Concert auditions are nerve-racking for a singer even when you know you are performing well, but I found trying out for Broadway musicals even worse. Casting directors have a variety of preconceived notions. Usually they are looking for a blonde—I am brunette—or for someone short—I am nearly six feet tall in heels—or a soft-shoe dancer—I studied ballet for years. I performed in a few summer stock musical shows that never made it to Broadway, and I sang many concert tours on the East Coast. Then in 1935 what I thought was going to be the big break came.

I read that Max Reinhardt was casting an extravaganza, *The Eternal Road,* the story of the faith, tribulations, and determination of the Jewish people. He had been an idol ever since I had seen *The Miracle* in Cleveland, and I was ready to take almost any part in order to work under this great impresario. Thousands of singers auditioned and you can imagine my exultation when Reinhardt himself picked me for the role of Rachel because he thought my coloratura voice, with its accuracy and bell-like overtones, was exactly right for the part. Unfortunately, the show was plagued from the start with production and financial woes. Meyer Weisgal served as producer and Max Reinhardt was the director. Kurt Weill, who was the popular composer of *The Three Penny Opera,* wrote the music, the well-known author Franz Werfel wrote the text, and the great craftsman Norman Bel Geddes undertook the setting, costumes, and lights. One would think such a team would have only smooth sailing. Quite the opposite was true.

Reinhardt, of course, was famous for breaking the conventions of theater, in such ways as replacing the proscenium arch and wall with vast cathedral interiors, circus trappings, and Greek amphitheaters. He thought drama should live for the contemporary viewer. The dramatic atmosphere he envisioned for *The Eternal Road* called for a complete rebuilding of the opera house stage area. While it was being transformed from the basement up into a five-level graded floor which terminated in a pinnacle at the back, the producers ran out of money. The original budget of $230,000 was not nearly enough and the opening of *The Eternal Road* was postponed at least ten times.

The rehearsals, when they took place, however, were marvelous. And my role was vocally challenging, for Rachel sang some very difficult passages and talked others in a singsong voice. In my finale of the original score, I held a resonant high B, spinning it out to a fine diminuendo as I walked slowly down the road, around some rocks, and descended into history and then faded away into the shadows of the wings.

There were hundreds in the cast. Sam Jaffe, Sam Goldberg, Sidney Lumet, Katherine Carrington, and Rosamund Pinchot, whose father was Governor of Pennsylvania, were among them.

When the 1936 premiere was canceled, the whole concept of the play was revamped. The new plan used fewer singers on stage and much of the music was prerecorded. Where live music was used the conductor and some singers were enclosed in a chamber with a glass front facing the stage. The soloists and the conductor wore earphones to follow cues. The singing role of Rachel was eliminated. An actress was given the Rachel role, and I was put into a chorus which appeared on stage from time to time to emphasize action. I had a solo, however, as one of the Heavenly Host, and I was also understudy to Miriam and Ruth.

The Eternal Road finally opened on January 8, 1937, and was well received. I was thrilled and in measure repaid for my efforts when *Time* Magazine mentioned specially my Heavenly Host solo. *The Eternal Road* ran less than five months and in the last weeks I played the part of Ruth. It had little singing, but after the musical closed, I was invited to represent *The Eternal Road* in a review presented at the

48th Street Theatre by the Understudy Club and I was asked to give concerts at the University of Connecticut and the Brooklyn Academy of Music by managers who had heard me sing in the play.

No intensive performing work is without its rewards, at least in experience, and in the summer of 1939 I was grateful for all those hours of rehearsing under the direction of Max Reinhardt when I was asked to be a principal soloist with the St. Louis Municipal Opera. The citizens of that Missouri city are enthusiastic about their opera company, and it is backed by newspapers, businessmen, and civic groups. I sang roles in such operettas as *Rose Marie, The Firefly, Katinka,* and *Babette.* An amusing and unnerving thing happened during a performance of *The Firefly.* I was singing the role of Sybil Van Dare who opens both Act I and Act II. Sybil appears very briefly once more at the end of Act I and she must change her costume between the acts. One night I put on the Act II costume without waiting for the second Act I entrance. I never had undressed, redressed, and run from the dressing room up the hill to the large outdoor stage so fast. That second entrance called for an excited voice. I certainly expressed urgency in my tones that night.

A couple of summers before I went to St. Louis, Helen Lewis, my roommate, asked me if I would be interested in substituting for the receptionist at Pan American Airways. Even at twenty-five dollars a week it seemed more profitable than another "Eleanor Searle Benefit Concert" in Plymouth, so I accepted, making arrangements to leave work early on Friday to sing for Sabbath evening service at Temple Israel. The company also gave me time off for important auditions. Ted Wyman, who hired me, was sensitive to the demands of performing artists, for through his cousin Dwight Deere Wiman, the theatrical producer, he was familiar with the requirements of the theater.

After the next summer I stayed on as permanent receptionist on the stipulation that I could continue with my church and synagogue responsibilities and could take time off for auditions so my musical career would not be hampered. I continued my singing lessons with coaches in the evening. The job was rather appealing. I greeted callers, took them to their appointments, and gave information to visitors. One of my tasks was to try to calm people when they had to wait a long time to see the top executives. Some of them sat impatiently in front of my desk all day, so it called for all sorts of conversational ingenuity. Occasionally I helped take messages from the teletype and decoded them.

Pan Am's commercial planes at this time were flying boats, which landed on and took off from water. Pan Am's aviation pier was on Long Island Sound at Port Washington. Often the company held parties in the hangars and I was invited to sing. It was in the course of my office routine and at those parties that I first met my future husband, Cornelius Vanderbilt Whitney.

Sonny and Juan Trippe had started Pan American Airways in the late 1920s. Sonny was a flyer in World War I and excited by the possibilities of aviation. After his discharge, the completion of his studies at Yale, and several years in mining he joined forces with Trippe and launched the airline to carry mail and passengers to Cuba. Many people roared with laughter at the idea that an airline could operate on a schedule and over water. But a group of investors were convinced it could be done and Pan American was born.

One of the executives was the calm and handsome Mr. Whitney. His sky-blue eyes were unbelievably clear, and he had an incredible, natural charm. I knew he was a member of the Metropolitan Opera Board of Directors and had backed musicals, and as an aspiring singer I stood in awe of him. We came to know each other gradually through our contacts at the office, musical events held in his home, and through informal gatherings of dinners and theater. As our friendship deepened and grew into love, I was troubled, for I was not sure I should marry a man who was divorced and Sonny had had two divorces. No one in my family and none of my friends had been divorced.

When Sonny proposed marriage to me in the spring of 1941, my head told me to wait a year. However, Sonny's mother, whom I had come to know and respect, told me she thought I would be a good wife for her son and she did not think that we should wait. And so I said yes to Sonny's proposal and to his hopes that we marry as soon as possible. I loved him very much.

CHAPTER THREE

My Life as Mrs. Whitney

UNLESS A MARRIAGE ENDS in heartbreak, separation, or divorce one does not go back to criticize and analyze the courtship. I thought that with the total love and affection I would give Sonny I could make up for his previous unhappiness.

In looking back, I do not think we should have married so soon. Sonny and I had not known each other long enough or in enough varied situations for marriage. We shared interest in music, horses, art, and the theater, but had little chance to see each other operating in the day-to-day world of grit and grind. I know that some romances which flower quickly turn into stable, lifelong marriages and I wish mine had, but almost always men and women need time to know each other well as persons before marriage, to become friends, to share ideas, to probe reactions. This did not happen during our few months of courtship, and I think now I should have taken the responsibility of seeing that it did. But maybe girls in love never do. I loved him, I trusted him, I said yes, and I committed myself to him for the rest of my life.

Our wedding date was set for June 18, 1941. The service was to take place in the Lutheran Church in Plymouth where I had been christened and confirmed and where I had often sung. Sonny and my parents had met several times and now he went to Florida to ask their permission to marry me. But there were no prior announcements, no rounds of showers, brunches, and dinners, and no advance pictures. Privacy is rare in the world in which Sonny lived, and we treasured it while we could by sharing our happiness only with family and our closest friends.

My apartment was the only place that buzzed with pre-wedding activities, and Helen, my former roommate, was my right hand in coping with all the details. She was particularly ingenious when it came to having the announcements engraved. She persuaded Tiffany & Co. to prepare announcements, leaving the names blank. When, on the day of the wedding, she gave the store our names, they completed the engraving and the announcements were mailed in pre-addressed envelopes. Instead of an engagement ring, Sonny gave me a ruby and diamond watch, and I picked out my own wedding ring, a traditional plain gold band. I could not even have our initials and the date of our marriage inscribed on the inside, but I never removed the ring from the day Sonny slipped it on my finger during the wedding ceremony until the day I was divorced.

A friend who was a designer made my wedding gown. It was delicate pink silk organza of Victorian simplicity, with full sleeves closing at the wrist, a fitted bodice and a wide skirt over matching taffeta. I wore a double strand of pearls around my neck, my wedding gift from Sonny, and carried a white bouquet of stephanotis and lilies of the valley. My veil was of chapel length arranged simply over my dark hair, which was swept up with a cluster of curls in the back. Since I am tall, I wore pink satin ballet slippers with ribbons crossed around my ankles.

In early June I went to Plymouth to help with the arrangements that had to be made. No one at home knew about the forthcoming nuptials except the family and the Rev. Richard C. Wolf, who was to perform the ceremony, and marvelously no one else learned until the night of June 17 when I told "Aunt Josie" and "Uncle John" Root. I had asked them a few days earlier to have luncheon with me that Wednesday, so on the 17th, the night before the ceremony, I told them the good news and asked "Uncle John" to play the organ for the ceremony. Sonny, his mother, and Roscoe Channing, an old friend who had helped Sonny found and operate the Hudson Bay Mining and Smelting Company, arrived by train.

Early on our wedding morning Sonny and I went to Mansfield, the county seat, for the marriage license. That was before the day of waiting periods. While we were at the courthouse getting the license, mother called friends, told them of the news and invited them to come to the wedding. Word spread fast in Plymouth on that warm June morning, and at high noon when I walked into the sanctuary on my father's arm, the church was overflowing. I was deeply touched by this expression of warmth and affection by the people of my hometown.

Roscoe Channing was Sonny's best man. My blonde, curly-haired niece, Katherine Eleanor Searle, was a flower girl and my only attendant. Following the ceremony we received our friends in the narthex of the church; this seemed to me to give our marriage a special benediction.

Afterward my brother George and his wife Mary gave a wedding brunch at their home in Mansfield. During the festivities the telephone rang and our hearts sank. In a family with two physicians, an unexpected telephone call usually means an emergency. But that day it was *The New York Times* calling to ask my father if it were true that his daughter had just married Cornelius Vanderbilt Whitney. Dad hesitated and we laughed as he thought about denying the report just to see what the ever-cautious *Times* would do. Then we had to remind him that it was indeed true—Sonny and I were married and the news media of the world could ring it out. They did. By the time we arrived in Cleveland to take the New York Central Railroad back to Manhattan that evening, the front pages of all the papers carried the story. The social, business, and entertainment worlds were amazed and excited, for we had kept our secret perfectly.

Scion of the Vanderbilt-Whitney Dynasty

I had known Sonny was well-to-do. I knew he moved in circles of important and well-known people. And I knew that he was descended on both sides from important historic families. But my husband's wealth and lineage seemed less significant to me than what he was himself. It was for himself alone that I loved him.

As it was, my husband was the only son of Harry Payne Whitney and grandson of William C. Whitney, corruption-fighting lawyer, Secretary of the Navy, railroad magnate, organizer of utilities, and builder of a fortune. The present Whitneys owe their wealth to him, but the family itself goes back to John Whitney and his wife Elinor, who came to Massachusetts in 1630 on the *Arabella,* the ship which followed the *Mayflower.*

William C. Whitney forsook his native New England for New York where he went into the streetcar business. According to rumor, he made forty million dollars in one decade. He married Flora Payne, the daughter of Senator Henry B. Payne of Ohio, and they had four children, two daughters and two sons.

My husband's father, Harry Payne Whitney, died in 1930, and so I never had a chance to know him. He was evidently a man of considerable yet often underutilized ability. He took great pleasure in camping and fishing at the family's wilderness estate in the Adirondacks. He played polo and tennis, and sat on boards of the Metropolitan Opera and the Museum of Natural History. He raised fine race horses, an interest which he inherited from his father who started the great racing stables in Lexington, Kentucky.

Sonny's father and his mother, the former Gertrude Vanderbilt, had known each other from childhood, as their houses were across the street from each other in New York City. Their wedding was one of the smallest but most important social events of 1896. It was held in the Breakers, the Vanderbilts' seventy-room summer "cottage" in Newport, Rhode Island. I have heard that her family was not enthusiastic about the marriage, but Gertrude was strong-minded; she would not be dissuaded and her family at last consented.

The Vanderbilts did not arrive on the *Mayflower* or the *Arabella*. They came to America in the seventeenth century, were first known as van der Bilts and settled on Staten Island in New York Harbor. "Commodore" Cornelius Vanderbilt, who died in 1877, founded the family fortune. He started out by hauling vegetables and people from Manhattan to Staten Island on a small boat and ended up owning a lion's share of the railroads of the East. Mamma, Sonny's mother, was his great-granddaughter; I think she must have inherited much of his energy and imagination and his ability to follow through on projects. Harry Payne and Gertrude Whitney had three children, two girls, Flora and Barbara, and one boy, Cornelius Vanderbilt.

Honeymoon Months

And so it was to the only son of two of the nation's great families that I was married on June 18, 1941. Like many newly married couples, we went to a secluded seaside resort for our honeymoon. Unlike most other couples, however, we had the whole place to ourselves. Sonny rented a private complex of cottages at Montauk Point on the extreme eastern end of Long Island. One building was for sleeping, another for eating, and more were for cooking, staff, recreation, and guests. Of course there were no guests, but Sonny did bring along part of the domestic staff from his Old Westbury estate. I spent a portion of my ten-day honeymoon having furniture moved from the various buildings so Sonny and I could eat, sleep, and relax in the same structure. It was the beginning of forty apartments, houses, camps, yachts, and an airplane that I would decorate and rearrange in my seventeen years of marriage.

After Montauk Point, we returned to my tiny three-room Tudor City apartment to pack my things and close that chapter of my life. Sonny owned a duplex apartment in River House on Manhattan's East Side, houses in Saratoga and Kentucky, and camps in the Adirondacks, but Old Westbury, Long Island, was home. That meant building a house, for the old William C. Whitney mansion on Long Island had been recently torn down. Sonny had had plans for the new house drawn before our wedding. The house was to be built on the foundation of the old mansion, but he wanted me to recheck everything so the house would be as I wanted it. We went to Old Westbury to be near the site, staying in Mamma's house briefly, then moving into the studio she had built on the property for her sculpturing. It was a Greek revival temple, and I think of it as our honeymoon house.

Although most of the property surrounding it has now been sold, the studio is still standing and remains within the Whitney family. It is basically one enormous room with a fireplace at each end. The floors are put together with hand-forged nails. The walls in the dining room were painted by Maxwell Parish in his typical brilliant blues, and the halls and stairs leading to the master bedrooms on the second floor were painted with portraits of Mamma and her friends in fancy dress costumes. Our bathroom was a sea fantasy, entirely dark emerald green with lumpy walls representing waves. The steps down into the large sunken tub were covered with raised figures of crabs and turtles and the sides and bottom of the tub area painted with fish and sea fans. Lights under glass in the tub made bathing like an underwater Jules Verne adventure.

When we were living in the studio our butler, cook, and waitress continued to live in a separate cottage by our new house or stayed in the New York apartment. It was probably the only time Sonny and I actually lived alone, and I was blissfully happy.

Turning an enormous studio into a livable place for honeymooners was a challenge. Since it was temporary, I did not want to buy furniture. We used some things from Sonny's old home and rummaged about in Mamma's storage rooms above the stables for others. I made a parlor setting around the fireplace at one end of the room and developed a music center around the other, delighted to have more than enough space for a Steinway concert grand piano. We used another part of the room for dining and left the center of the room open. It was splendid for everyday living and also for dinner-dances, especially since the front opened onto a wisteria-covered terrace and further to a garden where a series of pools led up to a cascading fountain. It was an enchanting place to begin a marriage; but the time was all too short.

War "Widow"

I no sooner had made the studio a comfortable place to live and turned to the details of building the new house when my world, and that of many other Americans, was shattered by the bombing of Pearl Harbor on December 7, 1941. Sonny enlisted in the Army immediately. He was commissioned a major on the basis of his experience in World War I. Sonny had enlisted in World War I, and although he had never been sent overseas, he became a top training pilot in Texas, the youngest licensed pilot in our nation. In 1941 our country was in great need of trained officers, and Sonny's quick response was typical of red-blooded men anxious to serve our country. He was stationed in Washington, D.C., assigned to a short course in Intelligence at Bolling Field. Not knowing where he might be sent, we stayed with his mother's sister, Auntie Gladys, Countess Lazlo Szechenyi, at 2929 Massachusetts Avenue. Houses were extremely difficult to find, and we were fortunate to have such a welcoming relative.

While Sonny was in training, I made a quick trip to Florida to see my parents as I always tried to do every few months. At the same time I was to receive an honorary doctor of music degree from Florida Southern College. My academic days at the institution were brief, but through the years I had returned there often to visit and sing. The main drawing room in the original dormitory bears my maiden name.

Sonny called me in Bradenton, saying that I should stay there since he was coming to Florida and would meet me at McDill Field in Tampa. The following weeks were among the most anxious and painful of my life. Knowing Sonny's love of action, his good friend Lt. Col. Merian C. Cooper had urged him to join a group under Brig. Gen. C. V. Haynes and volunteer for the first overseas battle mission of the war. A few of the wives came to McDill Field with their husbands. Of course none of us had any idea where our men were going, or why, or for how long. We knew that five Flying Fortresses stood on the field, that departure dates were continually set and postponed, and that we were in agony. The days dragged into weeks. We never knew what bleak sunrise would take our husbands away to some distant battlefield, perhaps forever. We lived in quarters at the field and ate in the officers' mess. Our attempts to bolster one another's spirit were never too successful. We wives picked up all the shreds of information we could by listening, afraid to try piecing the scraps together, and yet afraid of not knowing what the next day might bring. No wife dared to ask directly. Sonny intimated that South America was the objective, and I loved him for hoping to spare me pain, but I did not believe him. The war was not in South America.

I wept as I sewed name tapes in all his uniforms, socks, and gloves and labeled his equipment. And when I discovered that medical drugs were in short supply, I used what contacts I had to obtain painkillers and new infection fighters, such as penicillin. The medicine chest that I made would serve Sonny and his comrades well and eventually find its way to the Lady Wellington Hospital in New Delhi, India.

Those hollow days at Tampa seemed endless; the anxiety was crushing, and then the blow fell. Nothing, nothing will ever blot out the inner ache, the terror, of that final gray dawn on March 27, 1942. My parents had loaned me a car, and so I drove Sonny to the entrance of the airfield. All the others were aboard their planes and their wives had gone. Sonny and I were the only bride and groom, and we lingered as long as he could wait. Wives could not go on the airfield since the mission was top secret. I stood outside a high wire fence, watching him walk alone to the Flying Fortress in the far distance. He stopped at the foot of the steps, turned around, and gave me a proud salute. I waved and forced a farewell smile. With tears blinding my eyes I stumbled back to my car and watched the take-off.

I went "home" to Long Island. What home? I had no home there. The Neo-Greek studio was a honeymoon house. I was miserable in it without Sonny. Initially it was agony not knowing where he was; later the agony was in knowing the theater he was in and wondering what might happen to him. All the money and social standing in the world are no substitutes for the warmth and nearness of someone you love. I shed more tears during the next year than in the whole of my previous life. Many of the long letters I wrote my husband never reached him; there was no APO, for this was the beginning of the war and the communication system had not yet been set up. I would hear from Sonny through letters brought back by servicemen returning to the States. Later some of his letters came through the mail, filled with windows made by censor's clippers, but bringing love and comfort.

I do not think the military is wrong in keeping the details of hazardous missions from soldiers' wives. I was upset and depressed by Sonny's absence and I would have worried even more than I did had I known the goal of his mission; the objective of the men in the Flying Fortresses was a near-suicide bombing raid over Tokyo. Sonny was the Intelligence Officer for the mission; in his 1951 book *Lone and Level Sands,* he described the plan, and why it did not materialize.

Dinjan in northeast India was to be the first base of operation. A Flying Fortress should have made the trip from Tampa to Karachi, the staging site for Dinjan, in five or six days, but it took Sonny's craft eighteen days. Two days were spent in West Palm Beach with engine trouble. Then as they flew over Brazil a lifeboat blew out and caught on a wing stabilizer, causing five days' worth of damage. The *Snafu,* as the men christened her, mired down in sand at Kano, Nigeria, and in quicksand in Aden.

Once in Dinjan, Sonny and Lt. Col. Merian Cooper expected to proceed to an undisclosed airstrip near Hong Kong and to lay in the stores of gasoline needed for the mission. They were to be joined by the other four planes, bomb Tokyo, and then fly east with the hope of being able to bail out over Alaska. A danger-fraught expedition, it collapsed, as Sonny learned when he reached Karachi, only because the Japanese had captured the airfield at Dinjan.

As a result Sonny was assigned as Liaison Intelligence Officer to the Royal Air Force with the newly formed 10th U.S. Air Force in India under the command of Maj. Gen. Lewis Brereton. In June, 1942, General Brereton received orders to proceed to Cairo, with whatever bomber support he could muster, to try to halt the advance of the Germans across

the deserts of North Africa. The Allied campaign was success-
ful and Sonny was a part of the grueling victory over General
Rommel at El Alamein that autumn. While he was in North
Africa he was promoted to Lieutenant Colonel.

In order to keep my sanity during this lonely time, I continued my singing at the North Avenue Presbyterian Church
in New Rochelle and at Temple Israel, responsibilities which
were routine but still satisfying. I rearranged the apartment
in River House and tried to build the new house. Then suddenly a tragedy of inestimable proportions occurred. Sonny's
mother died.

"Mamma"

Gertrude Vanderbilt Whitney deserves a special place in my
story even as she was a special person in my life. Mamma was
the most remarkable public figure I ever knew and one of
my dearest personal friends. I am certain I could not have
endured those first days of separation from Sonny without
her. She was my confidante and counselor, a reservoir of
strength and wise experience. Mamma was fond of me; she
said she saw more of Sonny during our courtship and marriage than she had for years. She encouraged me in my singing, and she gave me sound and loving guidance in my
transition from struggling soprano soloist to her daughter-in-
law.

Gertrude Whitney inspired awe. I can see her now, standing erect and lovely beside the magnificent fireplace in the
chintz-filled drawing room of the home she and her husband
had built. She believed in discipline and raised her three
children sternly, yet her warm and sympathetic eyes were
filled with tenderness, sensitivity, and quick wit. An observant
newspaper reporter gave an accurate description of Mamma
on the day following her wedding in 1896:

Painting by Elizabeth Shoumatoff.

Nine years old.

High school operetta.

Beginning musical career, New York City, wearing grandmother's mantilla.

In the role of Ruth in Max Reinhardt's *The Eternal Road.*

Bride and groom.

With my parents at the time of my marriage.

Mamma (Gertrude Vanderbilt Whitney) photographed by Edward Steichen, 1937. *Courtesy of the photographer.*

With Lt. Col. Whitney shortly after his return from one year overseas in World War II.

With my son Searle, five days old.

Driving matched pair of hackneys in carriage with groom Walter Douglas.
Nina Leen, LIFE Magazine © Time Inc.

Reading to Searle.

Miss Vanderbilt is of medium height with rather slender figure. Her carriage and deportment are most graceful and engaging. She has a fine head of luxuriant brown hair which curls naturally. Her eyes are of grayish blue and her complexion that of light brunette. In manner she is most lovable, and she is a great favorite among the young people in her social circle. They like her because she is radiant in disposition and never puts on airs. She is an accomplished musician and speaks French and Italian with fluency.

Indeed she did speak French and Italian fluently, and she lived in Paris for considerable lengths of time in the early twentieth century. She had a beautiful studio there, which now belongs to her daughter and was recently used by Ambassador Averell Harriman when he was the United States representative to the Paris peace talks. Mamma did not, however, always remain a favorite in her circle, not because her radiant disposition changed but because she dared to expand the horizons of her world. In the days when ladies of her social station went fox hunting, did needlework, or sat for hours gossiping she was a doer. She deplored idleness as strongly as did my parents. She was creative American womanhood at its best.

Her first departure from expected norms was her insistence that she be educated in America. It was the custom of the late nineteenth century for daughters of wealth to study in England or France. But Mamma was taught history, literature, music, and art by tutors at home. Her education was thoroughly American, with the single exception of work with the innovative French sculptor, Rodin.

Mamma's greatest contribution to the American people was that of bringing American art to their attention. There were two interrelated focuses to this commitment: first, her patronage of aspiring American artists, and second, her own work as a sculptress. The first shocked the artistic establish-

ment; the second scandalized her friends. In 1900 no prominent art gallery or museum in the United States would
handle, sell, or show the works of contemporary American
painters or sculptors. But Mamma believed in America and
in the ability of its young to produce works of quality. Her
studio in Greenwich Village's Washington Mews became the
center of a new movement in the arts. She bought the works
of the poor and unknown to spur them on, introduced young
creators to each other, and presented them to her wealthy
friends. She gave scholarships for art education, provided materials, and commissioned works. Dozens upon dozens of
artists wrote when she died, saying they would never have
succeeded professionally without her support and encouragement. But she made no attempt to control the expression of
those she helped. Mamma was too much an artist herself to
bridle creativity.

By 1914 the collection Mamma had brought together in
the Village had grown so large that she opened the Whitney
Gallery on West 8th Street. The Whitney Studio, a meeting
place for artists, came four years later, and in 1928 both were
combined. Once Mamma offered her collection to the Metropolitan Museum, which, academic bastion that it then was,
turned it down. It is amusing that after her death in 1942,
the Metropolitan wanted to absorb the Whitney Museum of
American Art, but the public outcry against letting the
Metropolitan have Mamma's collection was so great that the
Whitney remained independent, first building its quarters
adjacent to the Museum of Modern Art on West 54th Street
in 1957, then when that became too small, building its
splendid new home on Madison Avenue at 75th Street in
1968. Interestingly, the Whitney Museum represents the only
art matriarchy in the nation, perhaps in the world. It was left
by Mamma in the care of her daughter Flora, Mrs. G. Mac-
culloch Miller, who is now chairman of the board of directors.
Her daughter Flora, Mrs. Michael Irving, is a key member of

the board. The first director was also a woman, Mrs. Julianne Force, a close friend and artistic colleague of Mamma.

Gertrude Whitney could identify with the frustrations and disappointments of young artists because of her own struggle to win recognition as a serious sculptress. I suppose the public was reluctant to believe a slender girl named Vanderbilt could be anything more than a perpetual dilettante. Her determination was considered bizarre by the elegant ladies of her family's social circle. The very idea of a Vanderbilt woman donning pants and climbing up a ladder to chisel at a piece of rock was strange, if not repulsive. But Mamma showed the same tenacious will about her career as she did on the question of marrying Harry Payne Whitney. She held to *her* decision. While the ladies of her social circle held crystal "hand coolers," Mamma sweated in one of her studios —in Greenwich Village, or at Old Westbury or at Newport— creating heroic-sized statues for public exhibition.

Today Mamma is recognized as one of America's great sculptors. That accolade was hard won. To keep people from saying she used the Vanderbilt or Whitney name to win commissions, she often entered competitions under assumed names. She worked from early morning to nightfall, accepting social engagements sparingly. Among her major works are the Titanic Memorial in Southwest Waterfront Park on the Potomac and the Mayan Fountain in the Pan American Union Building in Washington, D.C. In New York City there is a life-sized statue of Peter Stuyvesant at Second Avenue and 16th Street, and a War Memorial at 167th Street and Broadway.

My favorites are two enormous portrait sculptures: one of Christopher Columbus at Huelva, Spain; the other of Buffalo Bill, seated on a horse at Cody, Wyoming. The Columbus statue is across the river from Palos, marking the spot from which the explorer set sail in 1492 for what he thought would be India. It is about the size of the Statue of Liberty and was

a gift from the people of the United States to the people of
Spain. Columbus looks out to sea, his head hooded against
the wind and rain. His hands are folded over his chest in
such a way that his arms form the transverse bar of a cross.
His legs parallel each side of the upright beam. Though
made out of blocks of granite, the figure conveys a feeling of
youth, strength, and vision. It has a personal quality which
belies its monumental scope.

Mamma's concept of the whole event of Columbus' first
embarkment was comprehensive. She took account of Moor-
ish influences in Spanish culture, especially the importance
of light. The statue's 15-foot square base contains a room in
the center of which are life-sized figures of Queen Isabella
and King Ferdinand, seated on their thrones. Gertrude Whitney's sensitive artistic insight is shown by the contrasting
marbles she used for the king and queen; Ferdinand is the
darker and rougher, giving a masculine tone, Isabella is of
the smoothest, feminine white, and the monarchs are surrounded by an aureole of diffused light. One side of the
room has a wall map of the world in Columbus' day, another
wall lists the crew on the *Niña,* the *Pinta,* and the *Santa
Maria.* The names of the Americans who commissioned and
paid for the monument are on a third wall.

Mamma won the commission for the figure of Buffalo Bill
in a competition. The largest heroic bronze made up to the
time of its unveiling in 1924, Buffalo Bill is portrayed as an
Indian scout, mounted on his horse and leading the troops
along a ridge. As he looks down to the streambed he sees
Indian footprints, reins his horse sharply, and raises his rifle
as a sign to "halt," there is "danger." When she was erecting
the figure, Mamma became so impressed with the rugged
mountain terrain of Wyoming that she purchased acreage
around the site and presented it to the city of Cody as a park.
Today the Whitney Gallery of Western Art and the Buffalo
Bill Museum are located on the property Mamma gave.

There is a most delightful story connected with the sculpturing of this statue: it perfectly illustrates the scope and diversity of Mamma's interests. Among her many theatrical friends was Florenz Ziegfeld, the famed Broadway producer of the Follies and of the Midnight Frolics. One day in 1915 he mentioned to her that he had no suitable act with which to open his coming production. Mamma told him of a witty young man from the West who did rope tricks whom she was using as a model for her Buffalo Bill statue. Ziegfeld auditioned and hired him. Along with the rope work, the young man offered a commentary which kept the audience spellbound or doubled up with laughter. His name was Will Rogers.

Mamma had a depth of commitment to things she believed she should do. She never flinched; she chose her husband, sculpted, and championed unpopular and unknown American art and artists. In the time I knew the Whitney family before my marriage, and in the months between the wedding and Mamma's death, the fragile, shy, yet firm Gertrude had a profound impact on me. I cannot say that I ever considered trying to imitate her; this could not be done. Yet I was stamped by her values, similar in many ways to those embraced by my own parents. I have always hoped that I absorbed some of her gentle, humane forthrightness as well.

I was numb with grief when Mamma was stricken with an embolism in her arm on April 11, 1942. She died ten days later at the age of sixty-four. I was pained by my own loss, she had been such a support and friend, and I was distraught because I was unable to reach Sonny who was then in India. I tried to contact him through the Army, the War Office, and friends. I cabled, I wrote, I prayed. But he learned of his mother's death in an accidental way. He was chatting with Clare Boothe Luce, wife of publishing magnate Henry R. Luce and later United States diplomat, when she told him she was sorry about the death of his aunt—the radio had just announced the death of Mrs. Harry Payne Whitney. "But she's my mother," he said. My message with details arrived a few days later. Of course a soldier in wartime does not return even for his mother's funeral.

Building Whitney House

Longing for Sonny, crushed over Mamma's death, and wondering how I would face each lonely day, during the spring of 1942 I struggled ahead with the house in Old Westbury. The task was a tribulation almost matching my sorrow. I had never built nor thought about building a house, not even a simple house, and this one was to have twenty-four rooms plus great halls, breakfast porches, open patios, closed patios, two walk-in safes, storage, laundry, and pressing rooms. An architect had been engaged to plan and supervise construction, but although the exterior was of an attractive colonial design, the interior was extraordinarily inconvenient. From a housekeeping point of view, all the doors were hung on the wrong side—or swung the wrong way—and none of the electrical outlets were located where they would be needed; in some rooms all of them were placed along the same wall.

Supervising the construction under these conditions was emotionally exhausting as well as hard work, made harder because of the difficulty of getting materials in time of war. Lumber came from our own Whitney Park in the Adirondacks. We cut carefully selected primeval pine trees, sawed them in our own mill, seasoned them in the lake, kiln dried them, and had them transported to Long Island. The clear knotless boards—some up to 36 inches wide—were finished to preserve their natural color and were used as paneling in the library. Master woodworkers carved dentals at the cornice and acanthus leaf designs over the pilasters by the bookshelves. The pine boards we used for flooring, however, were a disaster, for I found that our pine was too soft to withstand the hard wear a floor takes. We should have taken oak such as my grandfather cut from his forest for my parents' home. Near disasters also occurred in the matter of plumbing. Of course, it was impossible to get new pipes and fixtures during the war, and so I had to scavenge about for sinks, tubs, and toilets and eventually used many of the beautiful Myer Sniffen gold bathroom fixtures from the old house. I also had to search hard for the mantels for the eleven fireplaces.

My best times at the building site had been when Mamma had come and climbed around with me. But now she was gone. Sometimes I tried to cheer myself up with pleasing discoveries in the vast Whitney storerooms. For instance, I found a cache of exquisite hand-painted Chinese wallpaper in the stable loft and knew it would be perfect for the dining-room walls. The very thin rice paper was in terrible condition, and so we soaked it in washtubs, pulled it gently apart, and hung it over wires to dry. It took months to piece the unrepeating bird pattern together. One peacock defied re-creation until it was discovered that he was looking under one wing, his head at the rear instead of in the usual place. Unfortunately, there was insufficient paper for the job, so I had to buy an enormous breakfront and design an elaborate mantelpiece wall to cover the bare spots.

And so I climbed over scaffolding, hung wallpaper and nailed up door facings and rooted about in junkyards, cellars, and attics, wondering why I was building that house. Would Sonny like it? If he did not come home I knew I would never want to live in it. It became the symbol of my anxiety about Sonny's safety. I felt that somehow he and I were being drawn closer and closer to an unknown precipice. And I deliberately isolated myself as much as I could in the studio and wept.

Occasionally, I escaped the problems at Old Westbury by spending a few days in the city at our River House apartment which overlooked the East River. Although my loneliness did not leave me there, I could put the pressures and dis-

couraging difficulties of housebuilding out of my mind more
easily. But the military convoys moving up the river brought
the war vividly into my life. There were many, many convoys,
for at that time troopships avoided attack in the open waters
of the Atlantic by traveling up the East River through Hell
Gate and into Long Island Sound, clinging for as long as
possible to the New England coast as they sailed eastward to
the European theater of war. The decks of the ships seemed
to be level with my windows. I do not sleep soundly, and
during this time of suffering I was usually awake from 3:00
A.M. to 6:00 A.M. I would sit in the bay window of our upstairs parlor, weeping and writing to my husband while the
dawn painted the eastern sky. The ships passed so near my
window that the thousands of young men lining the rails
looked close enough to touch. I waved at them and for a
moment smiles would break the empty stares of their young
and innocent faces. I wonder how many of them smiled for
the last time at an American woman as they passed my window. A desperate feeling seized me as I saw our manhood
sailing away from their homes and their country. It would
have been easier to have gone with them than to remain at
home, pretending to lead an ordinary life, trying to be cheerful, or at least patient, knowing that I was utterly helpless
where the only concerns of my heart lay.

As the first anniversary of my wedding approached, I realized that I must get the upper hand over the new house which
was, after all, an inanimate structure, not a living threat. So
I decided to spend our first wedding anniversary night, June
18, 1942, in what would be our bedroom regardless of how
unfinished it might be. Our bedroom wing was one of the
nicest features of Whitney House. It was not new. Sonny had
bought a fine early nineteenth-century dwelling in Roslyn,
an old port town north of Westbury, and had had it moved
to our farm. The house was white clapboard with a simple
portico of square wide board pillars which supported a two-

story porch. The windows facing out on the verandas opened down to the floor and could be used as doors, and the sun coming through them flooded the rooms with light. We called it the Kirby Wing after the sea captain who had built the original house on Long Island Sound.

Relocated and remodeled, its ground floor became our drawing room. The upper story was made into our bedroom, a dressing room and baths for each of us, and a small kitchen. I asked the carpenters to do what they could to finish the bedroom before June 18. They swept the sawdust out, and I steeled myself to sleep there on a folding cot. I shall never forget arriving there that evening. I expected the bleak skeleton of a half-finished room, and was greeted instead by great bouquets of flowers and a real bed. My sisters-in-law Flora and Barbie and another friend felt I should not stay in the house but, since I insisted, had as a surprise effected this cheerful heartwarming transformation. Their thoughtfulness went a long way toward helping me overcome my antipathy to the cold and empty structure. I began to stay in it more and more. That first night I sat up late writing to Sonny, telling him what his sisters had done for me, for us. Their sensitivity and imagination remains one of my treasured memories and I think today is an example of what Jesus means when he calls upon us to give, as a freewill offering through him, help, support, and love to our fellow human beings. Life without these expressions of caring is very poor indeed.

In 1943 Sonny was reassigned to the United States. He left North Africa at the end of February and arrived at La Guardia Airport in early March. There is no way of describing the immense joy of his safe return. It did not entirely erase the months of suffering and waiting, but when I saw him with my eyes and could touch him with my hand I knew that somehow I had come through that agonizing time and that at last together we would start making a new life, not as honeymooners but as man and wife, seasoned and brought closer to each other by the trials of separation.

That life, as it turned out, was not to begin in the house at Old Westbury, the building of which had so exasperated and frustrated me, but in Washington, D.C. The war was far from over and Sonny continued to serve his country, working in the Plans Division of the Air Force Staff which had offices in the Pentagon.

CHAPTER FOUR

Washington—Old Westbury—Washington

THE HAPPIEST YEARS of my marriage were spent in Washington, D.C., those last two years of World War II when Sonny continued his work on the Air Force Staff and the nearly three years at the end of the 1940s when Sonny was first Assistant Secretary of the newly formed Air Force and then Under-Secretary in the Department of Commerce. That happiness stemmed, in large measure, from the fact that my husband was occupied in Washington with responsibilities worthy of his time and energy. Along the road of life, as poet W. H. Auden has so rightly said, we have "the Time Being to redeem from insignificance." Many other duties, some pleasant and others not, must be carried out, yet if we do not redeem "the Time Being from insignificance," which we can do with help from the Lord, we cannot possibly be happy or contribute to the welfare of our world. Redeeming the time being, the present, means putting our ability and energy into something that needs doing, things such as alleviating suffering, helping the unfortunate, serving one's nation or, as I stress today, helping others to open their lives to the power of God so that he can work his love through them. Our years in Washington provided Sonny with the opportunity to give truly needed service to our country.

Those years, I think, were especially fulfilling ones for both of us. Just having a job, any job, is not quite enough. Real joy in work comes when the job is necessary. In spite of her great wealth, Sonny's mother knew this as did many of his forebears, and it was the rule by which I was brought up, so much a part of my heritage that it never even needed to be spoken of. Sonny was a vital, human part of the under-staffed Plans Division of the Air Force Staff. He worked long hard hours as the Chief of Projects and in 1944 was instrumental in shaping the Allied invasion of France and in planning the redeployment of the Air Force to the Pacific Theater of War after the defeat of Germany.

While Sonny was at his Pentagon office I was discovering the joys of keeping house and being a wife. We did not yet have children, but I did not want to take a job which would absorb the energies I felt our life together needed. I was happy with my role as homemaker.

I do not believe wives should work full time unless it is economically necessary. For the quality of family is too dependent upon their presence in the home not only to handle crises, but also to gather up the unheralded moments of joy and striving and even sorrow and transform them into means of growth and strength and cohesiveness. I do not mean that women should neglect their talents or bridle their interests. Rather, I recognize that a wife's or a mother's schedule needs to be flexible, responsive to the atmosphere of her home because this is her special creation. Work that allows itself to be accomplished within this framework is often an enrichment to the home. Mildred Bliss, wife of former Ambassador Robert Woods Bliss, constantly encouraged me to continue singing once we were settled in Washington. She told me she had been a violinist and had always regretted that she had put away her instrument after her marriage.

So, I followed her advice, practicing to keep my voice in condition and involving myself in the musical life of Washington. One of my major interests was the National Society of Arts and Letters. This organization was started in 1944 by Francesca Nielson and by Mollie Nicholson, a neighbor in Chevy Chase, to promote and encourage talented young people in all fields of the creative arts. I became a charter member and served on the advisory council for many terms. The Society's main emphasis is on scholarships and on providing opportunities for budding artists—dancers, writers, painters, sculptors, actors, musicians—to display their abilities. We announced our program in high schools and music schools, first only in the Washington area and then, as it proved its value, throughout the nation. Now there are chapters in many large cities of every state.

In my spare moments I gardened. Food was strictly rationed at this time. A housewife had to be extremely ingenious to provide an adequate and balanced diet for the family, and so we planted a "victory garden," some for us and some for the rabbits. Sonny would often pick fresh vegetables from the little patch, a couple of handfuls of string beans or a head of lettuce, and bring them to me as he came to the house from the garage after he returned from work.

I also spent many hours at Walter Reed Army Hospital. These were frequently heartrending, for I worked with amputees. Once again, as in Plymouth, I stood beside the bed to aid in the recovery of the maimed. Their condition did not shock me as it did so many others. I had seen the limbless before. Just because these men had lost their sight, legs, or arms did not mean that they had essentially changed. They were still the same persons with character, personality, and ability. Their great fear was that the people about them would now regard and treat them differently. I wanted more than anything else to do whatever I could to help them and their families adjust to life again. They were extraordinarily brave men, men who had given a portion of themselves for the welfare of our nation. I was always amazed that in spite

of their disabilities their morale was high. Perhaps one of
the reasons for their attitude was that they felt the undergird-
ing support of a grateful nation. Doesn't that say something
to us today? Sometimes I took a grabbag full of games, can-
dies, books, socks, and other small items and let them dig in.
Sometimes I brought great bunches of flowers, then I would
usher the mobile and wheelchair patients into a sunroom and
they would help me create colorful floral arrangements for
each of their rooms. Other times I took groups of ambulatory
patients to sports and musical events.

In the early fall of 1944 my visits to Ward Five came to
an end. I missed the afternoons there, but I had joyful news
for everyone; I was expecting a baby before Christmas. The
men of the ward gave me a wonderful farewell party. They
all wrote their names on a pillowcase and someone embroidered them in Air Force blue. The case, which I still
have, bears the Air Force insignia, and the words "from your
friends in Ward V."

I had not told anyone earlier that I was pregnant because
I had previously lost several babies by miscarriage, and just
before I announced the news, I gave a concert at Dumbarton
Oaks for the United Nations Fund. Imagine how surprised
people were when they learned I was to become a mother in
three months!

A Son Is Born

My clearest abiding personal memory from wartime Washington was my desire to have a child. The many miscarriages
I had were traumatic, debilitating experiences for a woman
who desperately wanted to be a mother. The doctors could
not discover why, at first, I did not become pregnant and then
why I miscarried so easily. All the usual tests and examina-
tions revealed nothing abnormal in either Sonny or me. Later
the importance of Rh-negative factor was discovered.

Because it was difficult for me to conceive and carry a child, I became interested in research on human cell reproduction. Sonny gave a grant for work in this field to The New York Hospital. Research was carried out by Dr. John McLeod, of the anatomy department at The New York Hospital and a leading authority on the human cell, on ways to keep a sperm alive longer by providing glucose energy in the path to the ovum. Some of the experiments were carried out on the brood mares at our Kentucky farm. As the experiments on the mares and horses proved helpful and potentially effective, they tried the therapy on me.

In 1944 I became pregnant and did not lose the baby. On November 14, 1944, at The New York Hospital a son was born to me and Sonny. We named him Cornelius Searle Whitney after Sonny and my grandfather, Cornelius Fenner. I had never been so utterly happy. My first look at the baby was the most glorious and joyful single moment of my life.

He was handsome, had dark blond hair, weighed seven and three-quarters pounds, and looked healthy and strong. But by the second day it became obvious that Searle was not retaining his food. His weight decreased substantially. The doctors could offer no explanation and, what was worse, they could provide no cure. "Your child is not going to live," one horrible specialist brought in for consultation told me. At first a mixture of sorrow, anger, and fear overwhelmed me. Since there was no apparent medical reason, I was determined that my son would live and I prayed. Fortunately, other pediatricians gave me hope and support.

I stayed in the hospital for two weeks while tests were made to determine why Searle did not retain food. I nursed my baby by holding him in an upright position. As soon as he lay down, he regurgitated. He reacted to all nourishment in the same way. He tenaciously clung to life, but grew weaker. Then at last, after several weeks, he improved and began to recover his birth weight. The doctors convinced me that my

presence near the hospital was of no positive value whatsoever, and so, torn and longing for my baby, I went back to
Washington to be with Sonny who needed me, too. A week
later I was able to bring my son to our home in Chevy Chase,
Maryland.

The final weeks of 1944 and many of the following years
were spent trying to discover what caused Searle's condition.
Several theories were advanced. A two-month stay in New
York Babies Hospital during which they pumped his stomach
and subjected him to endless tests, causing him to lose one-
third of his weight, produced the illuminating news that we
were experiencing a "feeding problem in infancy." I was
given all sorts of foolish psychological explanations. One was
that Searle vomited to get attention. In a seizure of omnip-
otence, another hospital nurse decided the child disliked
me and was vomiting to punish me. Ordering me out of the
room, she declared she would feed him and that no vomiting
would follow. She ordered me to watch through a crack
in the door. I was jubilant when he threw up all over the
bossy woman.

It was only after many years of observation that a sluggish
or atonic muscle at the junction of the esophagus and stomach
was found to be the cause of Searle's problem. He was not
in pain, but it was as easy for the food to come up as to stay
down. During those early years I was terrified to lay Searle
down. The pain of seeing my beautiful, handsome son unable
to gain strength and weight and the fear that he might choke
in the night were almost unbearable. He had tablets or liquid
medicine to take before meals, but in many ways, forcing
him to swallow them was worse than the vomiting. Yet in
spite of the constant tests Searle was a happy, responsive, and
active child. He never lost his sense of humor or his exuber-
ance. He has the same buoyancy and spirit of adventure
today.

In the midst of my anxiety I often felt utterly alone. Actually I was by myself for most of February, 1945, for Secretary of the Navy James V. Forrestal asked Sonny to accompany him to the South Pacific as the Air Force observer of the Marine invasion of Iwo Jima. From the rail of the *U.S.S. El Dorado* Sonny saw the amphibious units roll up the beach toward that bloody and decisive battle. They stayed offshore for about a week. It was a dreadful battle, alleviated only by this incident whose message is, perhaps, that even in the midst of war the past is always with us and that all are neighbors in the community of men. One day the Secretary and Sonny decided to thank the cook for his excellent services to them during that difficult time. The cook came up from the galley, and when he had been thanked, grinned broadly and asked Sonny about Yankee Maid, one of the great racing mares back in Kentucky. In his youth he had looked after her as a stableboy at Sonny's Lexington breeding farm.

Homes for All Seasons

Germany surrendered in early May, 1945, and shortly thereafter Sonny resigned from the Army Air Force. We returned to Long Island to begin residence in the Old Westbury house, and on October 5, 1945, we gave our first big party. It was to celebrate my birthday. Many friends from Washington came for the weekend for what amounted to a housewarming, though the house had stood completed for two years.

Searle was baptized later that month by Dr. Frederic Underwood, the rector of the Episcopal Church of the Advent in Westbury. This was the church to which the Whitneys had belonged for generations, and it became my church. Old Westbury at last began to feel like home.

The Whitney estate was a real farm and it functioned as such during the war. But it gained new life, especially in social dimensions, once the fighting had ceased. The stable which had stood virtually empty was filled with riding and driving hackneys, hunters, polo ponies, race horses, and Shetland and Welsh ponies. We also introduced a herd of champion Aberdeen Angus show cattle. The grounds and greenhouses flowered once again.

Over a hundred full-time employees were needed to keep the house and estate running. Most of the feed for the horses, Angus and Guernsey dairy herds was raised on the place by trained agronomists. The dairy was one of the few in the New York area that was allowed to produce raw milk for children or hospital patients not allowed to drink pasteurized milk. One health inspector said ours was the only dairy where he really welcomed a drink of raw milk. Special employees also looked after chickens, turkeys, ducks, guinea hens, and squab. There were maids of all types, butlers, housemen, cooks, grooms, horse trainers, stableboys, gardeners and greenhouse men, painters, carpenters, electricians, and men to maintain the sewage system and roads. All the work was supervised by a manager.

Sonny's sisters also had large houses on the property; it was what one might call a relative preserve. When Mamma died, Sonny bought his sisters' share of the farm and kept it running, including the various services needed for his sisters' homes. The estate was like a feudal manor, almost self-contained, a lovely, somewhat unreal world which eventually came to an end. In 1959 Sonny sold it to a land developer. The home I built is now the Old Westbury Country Club, and the stable is the New York Institute of Technology, the dairy and silo being used as dormitories.

I was particularly fond of the stable. I had grown up riding and driving, for my grandmother had a driving horse and ponies and my mother rode sidesaddle. Even after Daddy had a car to make his rounds, he liked to keep a horse. My favorite, of all the fine animals I have ever known, is still Larry, a high-strung and sometimes vicious stallion Daddy got from

Pete Lofland, manager of Plymouth's livery stable when I was still a little girl.

Pete had asked Daddy to put Larry to sleep because he was a wild West horse, kicking and biting anyone who entered his stall. But instead of killing him, Daddy bought Larry. He had learned to break horses out West and trained him beautifully, though the stallion remained spirited. I remember hearing Ed Curpen, the town jeweler, tell about seeing Daddy riding around the public watering fountain in the square one day when Larry decided to roll. My father jumped off before the horse could crush him, sat on the animal's head first one side and then, turning it, on the other, while its four feet kicked helplessly in the air. Larry never rolled again. Finally, the horse became so obedient Daddy would bring him home, unharness him, and say, "Go for your drink, Larry." The horse would trot to the fountain in the square, drink, then graze for a time along the railroad tracks beyond our house and come back to the edge of our porch.

When the weather was fine, I would as a very young child be lifted onto Larry's back and ride him down the lane to our stable. Daddy's friends thought he was foolish to put me on the bare back of that restless beast. But Larry never hurt me, not even when at age three I went into his stall and sat down under him while he was eating. When my distraught parents, who had been searching for me, discovered me and warned me not to move, I said, "Hi, Daddy," pulled myself up by Larry's front legs, and walked out between his rear haunches.

At Old Westbury, I especially liked driving my high-stepping hackneys. They were a pair of matched bays which had won both as singles and as a pair at Madison Square Garden. And I liked the headstrong Playboy, a polo pony which had been broken for driving but had never become totally reconciled to it. He plunged and kicked if you gave him his head, and succeeded in demolishing many carts. We had dozens of carriages, buckboards, governess carts, breaking carts, and many sleighs for winter driving, but I liked best the one-horse open sleigh in which Searle and I spent many crisp winter afternoons gliding across the open fields of the one-thousand-acre estate. In fine weather I often drove the matched pair to Westbury to do errands and to pick up guests at the railroad station. Somewhere there is a magazine picture of me driving a horse in my breaking cart. For a cover of *Life,* I was photographed sitting on the box in my carriage, with our beloved groom, Walter Douglas, sitting behind me. Walter had been at Whitney Farm since the days of William C. Whitney and often had driven him into New York City. In those days Walter had to stop and change horses in Jamaica; today we change trains there. The splendid groom worked for four generations of Whitneys and taught three of them to ride and drive, and I suppose he knew more about handling horses than any man on Long Island.

Only a few of the race horses were stabled at Old Westbury. The majority were kept at various race tracks. The breeding stock was kept in Lexington, Kentucky, where we went early each spring for the yearling trials. The only other time of year we used the cottage there was for two days in May for the Kentucky Derby in nearby Louisville. Our horses did well at the track in those postwar years, and often over the years the stable has been a leading money winner.

Unfortunately, I was not able to enjoy the horses as much as I would have liked, for my time at Old Westbury was almost entirely filled by supervising the house staff and keeping a social calendar that ranged from auctions of Angus cattle to dinner parties for Britain's famed Old Vic Players, tennis luncheons for our friends, and charity balls in the city. Sonny preferred not to have professional housekeepers, and so the entire running of the houses rested on my shoulders. A good deal of my time was also consumed by organizing the entourage for trips to other houses, travel abroad, or cruising on our little yacht, for Sonny always liked to be on the move. The trips on the yacht were not exactly a carefree vacation. In fact, yacht life for me involved being a combination galley slave and deck swabber. Other excursions were more of a holiday.

As long as my parents lived, we often visited them in their home in Bradenton, as we did in Plymouth. One of our favorite places to vacation in Florida was Marineland near St. Augustine. Sonny helped to start this, the nation's first seaside aquarium, in 1939. He told me that during the war, when it had to be closed and all the fish released, the porpoises stayed near the shore for days, waiting to be fed and seeming to long for their human companions. Marineland was reopened after the war, and we found it was an ideal place to visit with Searle and his friends during school vacations. There was a comfortable motel on the grounds, and the boys were free to play on the beach unsupervised.

But the main attraction was the oceanarium. There were portholes around the tanks where one could watch the divers going underwater to feed the turtles, porpoises, and schools of smaller fish. Feeding the porpoises topside was made into a regular show. They jumped twenty feet into the air to take fish from the trainer's hand, tossed rings to the audience, leaped through fiery hoops, pulled an aquaplane carrying a dog or a person, and "sang." We never got tired of watching their feats. The night feeding of sharks, twenty-foot-long sawfish, and other eerie denizens of the deep also was fascinating to observe.

We particularly liked fishing in the ocean from the Marineland boat which had a live well in it. When we captured a porpoise by harpooning it with a tranquilizer, we would hoist it into the well and bring it to the aquarium. We did the same with sharks, but they required an attendant to "walk" them continuously to keep the water flowing through their gills so they wouldn't drown. The attendant had to be alert, to sense exactly when the shark might wake up, so that he could escape to safety.

Substantial marine life observance and research was carried out at this center. The first "talking" of porpoises was recorded and their mating and birth were first seen here. I'm always impressed by porpoises' speed and gracefulness. Searle and his friends were sometimes permitted to feed them. The boys stood on a high diving board, holding eight-inch fish in their outstretched hands, and the sleek gray mammals with a mighty flip of their horizontal tails, rose straight up out of the water and with their smiling tooth-lined jaws, gently lifted the food from their fingers.

In late July or August we went to Whitney Park in the Adirondack Mountains in Upper New York State. It was a place dear to us. Sonny, Searle, and I were joined by Sonny's sisters and their families who had their own camps, and also by Sonny's older children, Harry, Nancy, and Gail.

The camps at Whitney Park were very rugged and simple. Our life focused on the out-of-doors. The children slept in tents amidst the blueberry bushes and adored it. They sailed, canoed, fished, and went on overnight trips, camping in cabins deep in the forest or in lean-tos of pine boughs beside the lakes. As they paddled silently along the water's edge, they could see beavers felling trees to build their dams, and they had great fun trying to steal up on swimming beavers to see how close they could get before the beavers, whacking their broad tails, dived and headed for safety. The children could always follow their route by tracing the little clusters of breathing bubbles that rose to the surface.

There were fish, mink, martin, and otter, too. And partridges dusting themselves in secret cleared places, and eagles sweeping the skies above the tall primeval pines, and loons giving the long eerie whistle and the piercing crackling laughs that proclaim their jesting lordship over the waters of the lake.

Deer grazed near the camp all the time. One summer we had a pet spotted fawn which we fed by hand with bread and milk from a bucket. And bears were particularly fond of our garbage. Many nights we used to drive to the dumps to see them feeding. Often they would bring their cubs—who tumbled and climbed up trees and then did not know how to get down. Coyotes had penetrated the Adirondacks and mating with stray dogs had formed a new breed of wild animal called coy dogs, which live in packs but seldom allow themselves to be seen.

One of our favorite parts of Whitney Park was a remote log cabin on Salmon Lake. Bill Touhey, a man with sparse red hair, freckles, and few words, was as near to a hermit as anyone I have known. He stayed in a guide house all summer as our fire watcher. Except for our visits, he never saw anyone unless he came into headquarters for supplies. His lookout was the top of a high metal tower, reached by a narrow, shaky ladder. The tower itself was perched on the bald granite outcropping of the summit of Salmon Mountain, a long and difficult trek up from the camp at Salmon Lake below. From his pinnacle Bill watched faithfully hundreds of miles of Adirondack forest. His only contact with the world was his telephone and his binoculars.

Life at Salmon Lake was like turning back the hands of the clock of time. We fished, chopped wood, and played cribbage in the evenings. I cooked on a wood-burning stove and even baked cakes in the oven, adding logs as needed to keep the temperature constant. In the early years ice for all the camps was cut from the lakes in winter and packed in sawdust to be used in the summertime in the old-fashioned iceboxes.

Our summers in the Adirondacks were interrupted by weekends at Cady Hill, the Whitney house at Saratoga, during the August racing season. Cady Hill is of the Victorian period with gingerbread trim and porches on both the first and second stories. It reminded me of my grandmother's house in Plymouth, so I redecorated it in an Early American motif, using some of the old glass and pewter and other pieces of Americana I had inherited from her. We always kept an American flag flying over the front door from the top balcony when we were in residence. The National Museum of Racing which opened in 1951 added to the interest of Saratoga for us. Sonny gave the major address at its inauguration and loaned many paintings and statues of famous Whitney horses as well as gold cups and other trophies.

More than Charity

One of the major privileges and responsibilities as Mrs. Whitney was to participate more fully in philanthropic work. This I welcomed. I was one of the first supporters of the Spoleto Music Festival in Italy directed by my friend Gian-Carlo Menotti. I helped many other causes, including the Musicians Emergency Fund, the New York Women's Infirmary, the American Cancer Society, the April in Paris Ball benefiting French and American hospitals, the March of Dimes, the Police Athletic League, Goodwill Industries, and The Medical Passport Foundation, Inc. The purpose of this last organization, founded by Dr. Claude E. Forkner and which I hope someday will become universally accepted, is to keep full and accurate medical histories. Through them the private physician or hospital can record each immunization, illness, operation, allergy, and so forth. A copy is given to the patient. This is particularly important today when so many families move, change doctors, or travel. It is well known that many misfortunes which could be avoided result from inaccurate and incomplete medical histories.

I served on a variety of executive committees and also arranged theater parties and house tours and fashion shows to benefit educational institutions and medical research. Frequently, I was asked to model or to sing. I have had a sustained interest in the Women's Auxiliary of The New York Hospital and the Salvation Army, and for over twenty-five years I have been on the board of the Travelers' Aid Society. Travelers' Aid places hundreds of volunteers and case workers in railroad, ship, bus, and air terminals in every large city. It gives information and guidance to the drifter, the runaway, the immigrant, the job seeker. It helps solve the special problems of the ill and the elderly. It assists tourists who have lost their pocketbooks and mothers who are overburdened with babies and baggage. At a time when more and more of our population is moving or traveling from city to city it provides a vital and constructive service.

Sonny continued the philanthropies which had been supported by his father and grandfather before him—especially the Museum of Natural History and the Metropolitan Opera. Sometimes he took an interest in specific projects, such as the maternity wing for the Community Hospital at Glen Cove which was built in memory of his mother. Our contribution for that came from a most unusual source, the sale of a historic book which means more to me now than it did in 1946. Mamma had left to her three children the Vanderbilt family copy of the Bay Psalm Book, the first book printed in America. There are only eleven known copies of the 1640 volume and ours was said to be the only perfect copy in private hands. The family together decided to auction this valuable book at the Parke-Bernet Galleries as their contribution to the hospital fund. At the last minute Sonny had a change of heart about letting it go and bid up to $150,000 in hopes of getting it back. But it went to another bidder for $151,000, the largest sum paid up to that time for a book. It is now in the Library at Yale University.

Because the Bay Psalm Book was important in American

history and because of its intrinsic beauty, I felt extremely nostalgic about it. I especially liked the lyrical flow of the Elizabethan English and kept copies of some passages. The wording of the 23rd Psalm is typical of the cadence and style. The song begins:

> The Lord to mee a shepheard is,
> Want therefore shall not I.
> Hee in the folds of tender grasse,
> Doth cause me down to lie;
> To water calme me gently leads,
> Restore my soule doth hee.
> He doth in paths of righteousness
> for his name's sake leade mee.

Those words sounded pretty to me in 1946; today they are the assurance by which I live.

Sonny and I also worked together on a special project at the Museum of Natural History. Even before we left Washington in 1945, we were planning the renovation and modernization of the displays in the Whitney Bird Hall which had been started by William C. Whitney. The project was directed by Dr. Robert Cushman Murphy, a leading ornithologist and conservationist. We redesigned the panoramic scenes in which the birds, many from remote parts of the world, were mounted in natural attitudes so that they seemed caught in a moment of life in their actual habitats. Curved, painted backgrounds were given enhanced authenticity by the addition of such objects as real grass, moss, branches, berries, and bugs. The lighted cases looked like jewels against the dark burgundy wall coloring. Involved interest in the Museum always seemed to me an extension of the family's deep ties with the world of nature which they enjoyed so much at Whitney Park.

Philanthropy to me is more than charity; it is also more than the attempt of those with wealth to honor their own names with monuments of stone and plaques of bronze. I have known rich, selfish people, but in my experience, most persons who earn, inherit, or marry fortunes feel a responsibility to finance educational and artistic projects that in some special way benefit the whole of society, improve and beautify it. True philanthropy requires the same care, sense of perfection, and commitment as does the pursuit of a professional career. It also requires a good measure of judgment and selflessness.

The refurbishing of the Whitney Bird Hall worked out marvelously. I wish I could say the same of my music school building at Florida Southern College, a project that was particularly close to my heart. Anxious to improve and enlarge the music program in Lakeland, I arranged for Dr. Robert Gayler, the director and organist from the New Rochelle church, to become the dean of the proposed Eleanor Searle Whitney School of Music. I fully intended to construct facilities to house the program he would direct. Large and small recital halls and practice rooms were planned.

Originally, Florida Southern was a college with colonial style architecture, but around 1935, Dr. Ludd M. Spivey, the president, decided that it would be a good place to immortalize the work of the modern architect, Frank Lloyd Wright. He persuaded philanthropists to commission Wright buildings, and soon structures with overhanging protuberances and covered corridors and esplanades began to invade former orange groves. So that it would harmonize with the other new buildings, my music school also was to be designed by Mr. Wright. A long, involved, and often comical relationship with the architect ensued.

The late Frank Lloyd Wright made valid contributions to modern architecture with his "organic" style. He attempted to enfold the natural elements, to harmonize buildings with environment and purpose, and to introduce new concepts of habitable space. He did much to bring the outdoors to the indoors. Personally, I think he also brought in too much sand

and rain along with the cactus and philodendron. Sometimes his buildings are not as functional as intended. This was made plain to me by his design of the chapel at Florida Southern. Singing in the chapel is a catastrophic experience for the singer and I would imagine for the congregation as well. Mr. Wright arranged that the choir be placed behind a partition of variously shaped openings in the concrete block wall. None of the gaping holes are at head height. When a solo is performed, the audience sees nothing but a heaving torso, which in a white surplice looks like an unsteady balloon. Whenever I sang there, I stood on an orange crate so that my head showed through one of the openings and my legs appeared in another hole below. I hoped that my notes would project to the congregation beyond the concrete wall.

I wanted the music building to be solid, functional, and beautiful, and, having seen the earlier results of Mr. Wright's pencil, approached the project with cautious deliberation. The plans went back and forth until the whole thing was as ludicrous as it was tedious. I would ask for simple line drawings of changes I had proposed and would have to wait months before I was presented with another watercolor sketch with my name emblazoned across it. A naïve sponsor might be impressed by such show, but I certainly was not. Neither was I uninformed on the qualities of a good concert and dramatic hall. Mr. Wright wanted to put the orchestra on a balcony instead of the usual pit. I asked how singers on stage would see the conductor. He proposed that the conductor use a baton with a large light on the end. How difficult for the singers!

Neither did I comprehend the reasonableness of a concave floor in the auditorium which resembled the inside of an eggshell. The seats would have had to be on angles or, to compensate, every leg on each seat would have had to be a different length. Mr. Wright also planned about a dozen toilets for the building. That seemed excessive. "I really hope the music won't be that bad, Mr. Wright," I told him. Finally, it became clear that the architect wished to accept no more suggestions from me. I took his last plan to several theatrical designers for appraisal. The consensus was that $100,000 would be needed after Mr. Wright's structure was finished before a worthy performance could be held in the hall. With great regret I was unable to contribute a school of music building to Florida Southern though Dr. Gayler did bring new musical life to the campus. I continue to have warm relations with the college, have given many music scholarships, and have continued to sing there through the years.

A World of Fashion

I have always appreciated beautiful clothes. I remember the pleasure I had when I was growing up, trying on hats in Miss Briggs's shop, dressing up in finery from my grandmother's attic, parading about in my mother's dresses, and wearing costumes in school operettas. Mummy set a good example in variety and taste and especially color. Once I had a heavy wool coat made for me from an Indian blanket design. It had bright zigzags of black, red, and yellow on bright blue and a lining of yellow wool. It was a perfect coat to wear when I was cheerleading, for it was cold in the unheated basketball court on the top floor of our high school. I can remember flinging myself in utter abandon, long brown hair flying, in the *choo-choo, choo-choo* of the locomotive cheer!

Throughout my life I have designed many of my clothes. Of course when I was training for the concert and operatic stage, I was keenly aware of original, dramatic, and becoming styles. But always within a limited budget. As Mrs. Whitney, I could spend a great deal on clothes. But the first year of my marriage I was in mourning for my mother-in-law, and while supervising the construction of the house, I was seen more in dungarees than in Paris fashions. Then, too, no one wanted to spend time and energy on fashion while the war was going on. It was only after we returned to Old Westbury from Washington that I was fully baptized into the world of salons and fashion benefits.

Fortunately, I am slim and tall; so I was often invited to model new fashions for charitable events, and I always enjoyed doing it. My first such assignment was in late 1945 or 1946 at a benefit ball at which Elizabeth Arden showed her new collection of haute couture fashions. Flanked by two Russian wolfhounds on diamond leads, I wore a white satin beaded gown and the sparkling diamond tiara which had belonged to the Empress Josephine and which had been loaned for the event by Van Cleef & Arpels, who still own it and display it frequently in their Fifth Avenue window. During the ensuing years, I modeled scores of times in person and in newspapers to benefit the charities to which I was committed. Each year the *New York Herald Tribune* devoted an entire rotogravure section to advertisements which benefited the New York Women's Infirmary and had well-known ladies pose. For many years Charles Revson, the president of the Revlon Company, asked me to be photographed for his popular beauty products. These charity events raise vast sums which are used to support much-needed humanitarian and cultural organizations.

It is well known that many women of wealth spend large sums of money for their everyday costumes, especially when they patronize top designers. But, while it is true that one may pay more for the name designer than for yardage of fabric, I know few rich and elegant women who throw discretion to the winds when they are buying. Good designs by houses such as Givenchy, Mr. John, Dior, St. Laurent, Geoffrey Beene, Tina Leser, Elizabeth Arden, Galanos, Mainbocher, and Charles James tend to stay in style longer or to return to fashion in the future. For instance, in 1971 I can again wear some of the suits, dresses, and coats designed for me in the late 1940s and 1950s. The creations of Giorgio di

Sant' Angelo are for the moment—they are pure fun clothes, colorful and happy.

My special fashion flair lies with hats. After receiving the "best hatted" award of the American Millinery Institute for many years, I was retired to the hall of fame in 1959, receiving the first "Gold Hat" Award of the Institute as the best hatted member of society. People are often curious about the "Gold Hat." Used as a locket or charm, the award is a one-and-one-half-inch-wide golden disk in the shape of a wide-brimmed hat with a twisted band of gold wire around the edge of the brim. The base of the crown is encircled with pearls, and there is a small diamond mounted in the center. The crown lifts and inside is the *real* "Gold Hat," a tiny replica of a wide-brimmed Texas sombrero.

Today, few women have their dresses designed and made to special order, for haute couture is too costly and too time-consuming, and most of the designers are making gowns to size. Excellent fashions can be found on the racks, with becoming and flattering styles available to everyone who wants to be well dressed at a fraction of the cost of an original design. There are no longer many women who fret about seeing their dress on someone else at a party. I have always felt that if another woman chose a dress identical to mine, it only proved that both of us had good taste.

"Best dressed" to me means wearing the most appropriate costume for the climate, the time of day, and the activity. My rule is, whenever in doubt, underdress. But I am delighted that we can do many things with colors and textures and jewelry today that would have been considered garish a few years ago, I guess because I have a bit of the gypsy in me.

Republican in Democrat's Clothing

When in 1947 the Air Force became a separate service and Stuart Symington, the present Senator from Missouri, became the first Secretary of the Air Force, he offered Sonny the position of Assistant Secretary. This was an honor for Sonny and I was happy when he accepted. I believe very strongly that citizens should always contribute to the welfare of the nation in every way in which they are equipped. It seems to me that America would have more citizen participation if we realized the advantages—absent in so much of the world—that our country offers. And I think each of us has a duty to serve our government, not merely in the military when that is tragically necessary, but by responding actively to the civic and community organizations that support and encourage democratic processes. Committed involvement of our energy and our money is vital. Perhaps greater understanding and pride of our country and deeper appreciation of our privileges as Americans would be generated if everyone could serve one year in the government here in America or in its agencies abroad as a normal part of our schooling.

In the years immediately following World War II the Air Force held a new prominence. It was a time of military re-evaluation and Sonny was anxious to see that the U.S. did not dissipate its air strength as it had after World War I. He was a member of the President's Air Coordinating Committee, the Committee on Civilian Components of the Defense Department, and administered Air Force business pertaining to the National Security Council, the War Council, the State Department, and such affiliate groups as the Air ROTC and the Civil Air Patrol.

Sonny served in what was referred to as the "Kitchen" or "Little Cabinet" of President Truman. The political atmosphere was as exciting as it was grave. The bi-partisan coalition which had backed President Franklin D. Roosevelt through the Depression and World War II had broken up. Mr. Truman's Fair Deal in domestic policy and his foreign-aid programs were meeting with opposition. The U.S. had been forced to assume the major burden of rehabilitation programs in Turkey and Greece which the allies had counted on Britain to shoulder. "Subversion" in the government was beginning to be discussed, the government of Chiang Kai-shek was tottering in China, and Southern Democrats were moving toward the Dixiecrat platform to protest the national party's liberal stand on civil rights. Many doubted that Mr. Truman could win the 1948 nomination.

As a lifelong Republican I was intrigued and also captivated by President Truman's ability to cope with huge problems. Today we might say he knew how to keep his "cool." I personally do not believe our nation could have had a better man as President during the chaotic postwar period. He had vision, he had spunk, and most of all, Mr. Truman had extraordinary courage. He was earthy and strong. Mrs. Truman, his constant and loving support, was an example of what every wife should try to be to her husband.

The First Family was unusually gracious to us, including us in many private and semi-public social events at the White House. When the lengthy rebuilding and refurbishing of the Executive Mansion was finished, Mrs. Truman gave me a personally guided tour. Barbie, my sister-in-law, came with me. Mrs. Truman showed us specially the little cactus garden in the top floor solarium which I had sent her from Arizona the Christmas before. Because of shared musical interest, Margaret Truman—now Mrs. Clifton Daniel—and I became friends and have often served together on committees.

Perhaps the most exciting experience during this period came when I was asked to sing the National Anthem at the final session of the 1948 Democratic National Convention in Philadelphia. I had to be in Old Westbury that morning, and so I chartered a small plane to fly me to the City of Brotherly Love. The charter company assured me that the pilot enjoyed a brilliant war record. He did indeed. The problem, as it developed, was that having just returned from Europe, he had never flown the New York to Philadelphia route. I ended up reading the chart on my lap as the little two-seater lurched and tossed and bounced on the hot air currents wafting up from the New Jersey oil refineries. We were approaching the Philadelphia area, looking anxiously for landmarks, when both the pilot and I noticed a large number of Navy planes buzzing us in frighteningly close maneuvers. I wondered if a soloist for a Democratic Convention always received such a spectacular welcome!

We had started to land on the runway below when a crackling, angry voice through the headphone brought us up short: "Get out of here. You're a civilian plane and cannot land at a restricted naval air station." The poor pilot pulled the stick back, we were in momentary air limbo, and began again our search for the commercial field. He was as concerned as I was that I would be late to the convention hall. He also wanted to get us both there alive. We were enormously relieved when at last we located the municipal airport, landed, found the private plane entrance, and taxied in. I sprang from the plane and commandeered a taxi. More surprises at the convention hall. I didn't have proper credentials, and even though I pleaded that I was the awaited soloist, the guards wouldn't let me in. Hot and tired, I carried my suitcase from one office to the next until Leslie Biffle, secretary of the Senate, came to my rescue. Leslie, that dear wiry man, procured a badge which allowed me to go anywhere in the building, stashed my luggage, and took me to the organist. To my initial consternation but eventual amusement, I discovered the organ console was several stories below stage level. The accompanist and I discussed the key and tempo in which I would sing, and then I exhaustedly climbed the dreary backstairs to the auditorium level. As I walked onto the stage, I was warmly greeted by the Speaker of the House, Mr. Sam Rayburn. But even his welcoming kiss and subsequent eloquent introduction did little to ease my concern as to whether the organist, four floors below, would be able to see my lips on closed-circuit television so that we could deliver the National Anthem with the precision and gusto it deserves.

As I smoothed my white organdy afternoon dress, appliqued with lavender, pink, and green flowers and gathered by a black velvet corselet, and walked to the podium, I felt a surge of national pride. I remembered the times I had stood by my father and mother watching parades; they always encouraged me to stand very straight and salute. Today I'm asked to sing the National Anthem for all types of organizations, and my spine tingles and my heart swells with pride every time. I think the words of the fourth verse are particularly stirring:

Oh! thus be it ever, when freemen shall stand
Between their loved homes and the war's desolation!
Blest with victory and peace, may the heav'n rescued land
Praise the Power that hath made and preserved us a nation.
Then conquer we must, when our cause it is just,
And this be our motto: "In God is our trust."
And the star spangled banner in triumph shall wave
O'er the land of the free and the home of the brave!

That night, against great odds, President Truman received the nomination. I shall never forget the parades, the demonstrations and fanfare, the excitement and exhilaration expressed by the followers who celebrated his victory.

I had stayed on the platform during the balloting, and after President Truman was nominated, visited with friends in their boxes to watch the parades. When it was over in the early hours of the morning, the Secretary of the Treasury, John Snyder, and his wife asked if I would return with them to the Capital. I was grateful; Sonny had hoped to come to the convention and, at the last moment, had been detained in Washington. I thought we would be driving, but the car took us to the station in a procession and we returned to Washington on President Truman's private train. The coaches moved slowly through the night so that all aboard could sleep, and when we arrived on the outskirts of the city early in the morning, our train was put on the siding to give the passengers still a few more hours' rest. But I could not stay asleep; I was too filled with thoughts, thoughts of a girl from a small town in northern Ohio who had sung the National Anthem at a nominating convention and was arriving in Washington's Union Station on the train with the President of the United States.

Although I am a Republican, I worked avidly for the Truman campaign in 1948, and kept restless vigil through that long November night when it looked as though Governor Dewey would win. The Truman triumph gave us all renewed energy and hope. It was time again for celebration. I plunged into plans for the Inaugural Gala, for which I was music chairman.

Life on the Potomac

Compared with the war years, Washington's social life was dazzling in the late 1940s. We lived in a suite at the Shoreham Hotel for about a year, moving in October, 1948, to a house on 30th Street in Georgetown, right behind the so-called Lincoln House. Actually, our home was three small houses combined in one. It had a sunken patio, a guest house, greenhouse, and a fountain in the center of the garden. We had enjoyed having our friends in when we were at the Shoreham, but gatherings at our own home were even more delightful. A random sampling of my guest books shows that we gave a buffet dinner before a benefit performance of the Ice Capades, having among our guests Margaret Truman, Gen. and Mrs. Dwight D. Eisenhower, and Gen. and Mrs. Omar Bradley. That night, too, I sang our National Anthem before the ice show started. Perle Mesta, with Chief Justice and Mrs. Frederick Vinson and Senator and Mrs. John Fulbright, were at another of our dinners.

One of our most memorable dinner-dances in our Georgetown house was for Vice President Alben Barkley in May, 1950. At that time Sonny was in the Department of Commerce as Under Secretary. We served the dinner in the garden and used different types of art objects to designate the seating arrangement. I chose as centerpieces a porcelain bull, crystal birds, silver trophies, and porcelain horses. The objects were intertwined with miniature ivy in practically invisible containers. Our flowers and fowl as usual came from Whitney Farm. That night the main course was our own home-grown squab. We were extremely fond of the "Veep" and his wife Jane. Her mother was a noted pianist and frequently accompanied me when I sang.

But all was not dinner parties and political campaigns. During the nearly two years Sonny was with the Air Force, I had various duties as wife of the Assistant Secretary. One was helping in the formation of the Auxiliary Air Force Women. As a token of thanks, when Sonny resigned from the department, the women at Bolling Field presented me with a red morocco music carrying case, which I still use. I sang many concerts with the Air Force Band, which then was under the able direction of Col. George Howard. Secretary Symington asked me to serve on a very small committee which designed the musicians' uniforms. I wanted the men of the Air Force Band to look distinctive, and we decided on bright electric blue jackets with stripes of the same color on dark trousers. The Air Force Band is superb.

Often we went to Sunday worship at the New York Avenue Presbyterian Church. I was always amazed at the lines of people on the steps and in the vestibule, waiting for admittance to the two morning services. The Rev. Peter Marshall, Chaplain of the Senate, was the minister. I regret that I was not sensitive enough to the importance of faith in those years to attend his Bible classes and to seek out a more personal friendship with Dr. Marshall and his wife Catherine. During more recent years Catherine Marshall has become not only an acquaintance but an inspiration for my own spiritual development.

Our philanthropies continued in Washington. We presented a Van Dyke painting of Henri de Lorraine, Duc de Guise, to the National Gallery of Art. I participated in raising funds for the National Symphony Orchestra, and each year Sonny and I were hosts to a group of high school students from Plymouth who came to get a firsthand glimpse of the government in action.

From 1949 to 1950, the year that Sonny was Under Secretary of Commerce, we traveled extensively, both privately and for the government. We spent most of September and October, 1949, in Europe where Sonny's job was to encourage tourism in the U.S. and to represent the country at the International Union of Official Travel Organizations meeting in Luxembourg. In Italy, we took a side trip from Rome, where my husband had been speaking, and went to the ancient city of Sienna. Since early times, twice a year, extraordinary horse races have been held there. Each section of the town picks its favorite mount for a no-holds-barred race around the cobblestone square. The corners of the buildings are padded so the animals will not rip themselves in the melee, and grandstands are built in the center of the square. On the morning of the contest the horses are taken into the cathedral to be blessed. The race is wild with ecstatic cheering by the crowds and dangerous riding by the jockeys. In the evening there is a victory banquet; the winner sits at the head of the table, not the jockey, not the owner, but the horse.

Another highlight of our European trip was being in Luxembourg when Perle Mesta presented her credentials as United States Minister to the Grand Duchess Charlotte. Perle invited us to stay with her even though her residence was not yet ready for guests and the freshly painted house reeked with turpentine. I helped her unpack barrel after barrel of dishes. On our second day there, she went to the palace for the presentation. It was strange to see Perle dressed in a ball gown and long white gloves and adorned with glowing jewels at nine o'clock in the morning. I had dined with the mayor of the city of Luxembourg the night before and had had the rare pleasure of telling him about Mme. Mesta, a woman so internationally famous that it was novel to meet someone in government who did not know her. Perle was a most popular minister, so right for mineral-rich Luxembourg. She is knowledgeable about mining and went on inspection trips down into the shafts with the workmen. While she was stationed there, she gave parties for thousands of our men in uniform, bringing them assurance that their service to our country was deeply appreciated.

To keep our friends apprised of our activities, I periodically wrote long, long letters that out of sheer necessity were mimeographed. One letter that I have recently reread told about an unusual gift I gave Sonny for his birthday in 1948. My husband's military career held special significance for him, and so I had designed a silver chest engraved with the signatures and insignia of the officers and friends with whom he served. The box is fourteen inches long, six inches high, and eight inches wide, and is a unique chronicle of the military leaders of World War II. On the top are the signatures and five-star insignia of several famous generals; it took me several years to collect them all. I began with General John Pershing's autograph, as he had been Sonny's Supreme Commander in World War I. I had received it in 1944 and was told that this was the last autograph he ever gave. I had seen him often at Walter Reed Army Hospital when I was a volunteer there. Gen. Dwight D. Eisenhower and Gen. Henry ("Hap") Arnold of the Air Force are also represented. Col. Robert L. Scott, pilot of Sonny's 1941 mission to India and author of *God Is My Co-Pilot,* gave me his colonel's eagles. Brig. Gen. Emmett ("Rosie") O'Donnell, Jr., now president of the USO, gave me the star he wore when he led the first bombing mission over Tokyo. Lt. Gen. Lewis Brereton,

Sonny's North African Commander, and Field-Marshal Bernard Law Montgomery cooperated, as did Maj. Gen. Jimmy Doolittle, the new Secretary of Defense James V. Forrestal, and the widow of Gen. George Patton who gave me her husband's autograph. William F. ("Bull") Halsey gave me the four-star bar which he wore as the Commanding Admiral in the Surrender Ceremony aboard the *U.S.S. Missouri* at Tokyo Bay in 1945. President Roosevelt's and President Truman's signatures are also on the box.

I very much wanted a five-star circle from Gen. George C. Marshall, who at that time was in China. I wrote to Nanking, explaining the project and asking for his signature and a metal button or other insignia. He wrote back, saying he was supplying the autograph, but that he had no insignia with him, the very buttons from his white uniforms having disappeared in the laundry. However, he sent a letter of authorization with instructions so I could buy the five-star circle to represent him. I felt that if a man of such importance could take the time to explain purchasing details to me, the least I could do was to send him a set of buttons, and so I did.

On Christmas Day, 1947, I received the following cable from the future Secretary of State:

> The proposition started with a request from you for insignia and autograph for a collection being made for your husband's surprise gift. It has resulted however in the delivery in far off China of a very handsome set of buttons for my white uniform. I am very grateful and deeply appreciative of your thoughtfulness. Also in sending Christmas greetings to you and your husband, I would add for his eyes only that I have definite proof of his rare good fortune in the choice of a wife. My best to you both.
>
> /s/ George C. Marshall

The most difficult part of this whole four-year project was keeping the unexpected cable a secret from Sonny, which would have ruined the surprise. Of course I showed it to him later.

The silver chest has resisted tarnish; human relationships are not always so fortunate. But in human life satisfaction does not come through possessions. The only way we can attain lasting joy and not become tarnished is to know our Creator. Blaise Pascal, the seventeenth-century French physicist and philosopher, once said, "In every human heart there is a God-shaped vacuum that cannot be filled with man-created things, but only with a relationship to God as revealed through Jesus Christ." When we left Washington in 1950, engrossed as I was in an everyday life that seemed rich and fulfilling, I was still many years away from knowledge of that truth

CHAPTER FIVE

"Mrs. Nicodemus Meets God"

WHEN SONNY RESIGNED from the Commerce Department in 1950, we returned to a life centered in our home and estate at Old Westbury and our River House apartment in New York. We went to the opera, entertained our friends, participated in benefits for charity, went to the races in New York, Kentucky, Florida, and California, cruised on our yacht, summered in the Adirondacks, and traveled abroad. In 1952 I attended the Coronation of Queen Elizabeth and spent a glorious week in London celebrating her accession to the throne.

My son Searle was attending the Greenvale School—its buildings are just opposite the entrance to Whitney Lane. I taught him to ride his bicycle and to swim, and we rode our horses together. For winter sports we built a snow slide as high as the roof of the house. We pulled our sleds and toboggans up the wide, low steps to the top for a roaring start down the half-mile run across the fields. Blackie, one of our patient ponies, adorned with Russian sleighbells and drawing long ropes, would wait for us at the bottom of the hill and pull us up again. We had skating parties on the pond in front of the house with bonfires, hot chocolate, and toasted marshmallows. We had garden parties and tennis parties in the spring and always celebrated the Fourth of July with a magnificent display of fireworks on the lawn.

Gail, my stepdaughter, spent as much time with us as she could, part of her winter vacations and a month or two in the summer. She was a lovely golden-haired young girl and Searle adored her. Nancy and Harry, Sonny's older children, were usually with us in the summers, too. I liked being a stepmother. My own mother had raised two stepsons and loved them as her own, and I had been partly raised by my half brother George, who was like a second father to me. I know the joy a spread-out family can bring.

As I look back on my life before 1957, I wonder why it had never occurred to me to find a thread of meaning in the varieties of experiences I had had, why I had not questioned to what purpose they might be leading. For only by looking back over your life can you see the pattern that illuminates the really important, the revealing moments. Those years held so much: a happy childhood in an American heartland state, adventures in Florida, the excitement of working in New York, a singing career, marriage to the man I loved, the grueling experiences of a war-wife, the birth of my son, political identity, travel, and, of greatest significance, constant, close contact and involvement with people of diverse backgrounds.

It did not appear to me that these experiences might serve a higher good. Today I believe that God intended that I be able to identify with a wide variety of people. That awareness did not strike like a bolt from the blue, but developed only as I progressed toward becoming a maturing, serious Christian, eager to invite others to accept God's gifts. In retrospect, I realize that all through my life God has been shaping me into a usable vessel. He can use anyone—the only ability one needs is availability.

One of the most relevant events toward which my life had been leading came to me in the summer of 1957 when I attended the Billy Graham Crusade in New York City. I think of myself at that time as a "Mrs. Nicodemus" coming face to face with Jesus and with herself.

Nicodemus is a character who appears several times in the Gospel of John. He is introduced in chapter three as a ruler of the Jews, a teacher of prominence and social position, a Pharisee who fulfilled his obligation to God by tithing and by praying and by obeying the Levitical laws. Nicodemus came at night to question Jesus—perhaps he didn't want anyone to see him talking to the controversial Galilean leader, but he seems to have been attracted by the new quality of life he saw in Jesus. According to the Evangelist John, Nicodemus started with a nice compliment, saying,

> We know, Rabbi, that you are a teacher sent by God. No one could do the mighty works you are doing unless God were with him. (TEV)

How like any of us when we are trying to entice another person to tell us something personal or when we are fishing without knowing just what we want to catch. Nicodemus evidently wanted Jesus to tell him his "secret," to explain how he performed miracles of healing and why so many people listened to him. Jesus must have seen into his heart because he responded to Nicodemus' motives rather than to his flattering remarks. Jesus replied,

> I tell you the truth: no one can see the Kingdom of God unless he his born again. (TEV)

Nicodemus thought Jesus meant returning to the womb again and was confused by this, but Jesus admonished him, saying,

> No one can enter the Kingdom of God without being born from water and the spirit. Flesh can give birth only to flesh; it is spirit that gives birth to spirit. You ought not to be astonished, then, when I tell you that you must be born over again. (NEB)

In this passage Jesus makes clear that the Kingdom of God is attained neither by personal moral achievement nor by good works, but by a radical transformation—a change or conversion wrought by God. In other words: All your knowledge about religion and your scrupulous attention to ritual will not save you, Nicodemus. Unless you are born of the spirit, you will never make it to heaven to be with God for all eternity. Judged by the religious and social standards of his people, Nicodemus was good, respected, wise, and politically powerful. But as depicted in the third chapter of John, he lacked the essential requirement for being a part of God's kingdom. He was not born of the spirit.

Prior to the Billy Graham Crusade in 1957, I was a "Mrs. Nicodemus." I said extremely complimentary things about God, Jesus, and the church. I went to services of worship. I sang in the choir. I said prayers. I devoted a great deal of time and money to good works. I had many close friends and literally thousands of affectionate acquaintances. And I had great love for and from my family. I was not learned as was Nicodemus, but like him, I had a desire to know more about God's love, yet could not ask the right questions nor hear the answers when they were given. I had a full, rich, endlessly busy, glorious life, but I was not an awake Christian. Whatever genuine religious feeling I had, I kept locked in my heart. It was isolated, encircled by an empty coldness.

"Welsh Rabbit" Religion

As I have told earlier, the church played an extremely important role in my childhood. A succession of Lutheran clergymen in Plymouth lived in the parsonage next door and were our closest neighbors. The ministers' children were friends and playmates. I never missed Sunday school or morning worship. I liked the church building, with its two steeples, entrances at each front corner, and the large stained-glass window between them. The ceiling had heavy, age-darkened oak paneling and arches with Gothic embellishments. I so clearly recall myself as a very tiny child lying in a pew with my head on my mother's lap—there was no Sunday nursery then—fascinated by tracing the patterns of all those lacy trimmings and delighting in the large wooden balls which hung where the horizontal and vertical support beams met. On the rear wall, high above the arches, was a mural of Jesus. There were clouds encircling him, and though I realize now it was a painting of Jesus praying in the Garden of Gethsemane on the night that he was betrayed, to my childish mind it was Jesus hanging onto the "rock of ages" with the waves dashing up on all sides.

When I was a teenager, I sang in the church choir, I was a member of the Luther League, and for a year was Sunday School Secretary. It was all very interesting and time consuming, a good way to be with my friends, but we never talked about having a close relationship with Jesus. In fact, my clearest memory of religion in Plymouth is of Welsh Rabbit. After Luther League I often invited my friends to come to my house for an informal party—it was a perfect way to ask boys from the neighboring towns. We would have a light supper with hot chocolate, sandwiches, and Mother's Welsh Rabbit. I don't remember a single program sponsored by the Luther League, but I do remember that Mother served the Rabbit from a silver chafing dish and that the chafing dish had long horn handles. I suppose I had a "Welsh Rabbit" religion.

I hope I do not sound disrespectful of the congregation in which I was baptized and confirmed and married nor of the ministers who pastored the flock in Plymouth. I know the men were devout, sincere, and good. And I certainly do not intend to be critical of religion in my home; we had grace at meals, and I was taught to pray. Often after Daddy had finished treating a patient, especially after surgery, he would explain that he had done everything he could and that the healing was now in God's gracious hands. But though we all had Bibles—black, forbidding editions with tiny print and drab covers—we never studied or even read the Scriptures together. Furthermore, I do not remember that anyone during my childhood talked about personal faith or about a personal encounter with God. Perhaps it was not the time—not for Midwesterners anyway. There were no challenges to let God take total control of your life in the sermons I heard, no stress on how to be "born again" into the kingdom of God's love through Jesus Christ. Jesus, to me, was a "sweet" little face in a picture, hardly distinguishable from the painting of St. Cecelia, patron of musicians, which hung over our piano —what a shame it is that most of the artistic representations of the Lord concentrate so much on "sweetness and light" that the strength of his love and the fierce joy of his forgiveness are left out.

In northern Ohio I never saw or heard of an evangelist, of a revival, of a public commitment, nor of any outward, joyful, or enthusiastic indication of faith in God. Religion was either just a cultural convention and ritual or considered entirely *too* personal to talk about.

"Of Course I'm a Christian"

The one challenge toward a personal relationship with God came to me as a teenager and was, I am ashamed to say, very embarrassing to me. I am thankful for it now, but I certainly was not when it happened.

During a holiday I was visiting relatives in New Hampshire. My cousin Marjorie Miles Campbell and Carlton, her new husband—he is now a surgeon—asked me if I were a Christian. It was the first time I had ever been pinned down by that question. "Of course I'm a Christian," I answered. They asked me how I knew. I'm sure I must have replied,

"Because I've been baptized and confirmed." Then they wanted to know *what* I had confirmed.

I could describe the service. I wore a white dress, felt all sparkly, and enjoyed the congratulations and gifts. To me confirmation meant I had learned the creeds and studied Luther's catechism. I *had been* confirmed, but had I *confirmed* anything? I do not remember anyone impressing on me the need for a living relationship with God. My confirmation vows and the service were only superficially meaningful to me. I did not realize that I was confirming that I loved God and that I knew Christ had died in my place so I could have forgiveness of all my sins, past, present, and future. Nor did I realize that I was confirming publicly my invitation to Christ to come and live in me with the Holy Spirit, that I was beginning a life as a citizen of heaven and from that moment would never be alone.

> Yet to all who received him, to those who believed in his name, he gave the right to become children of God— children born not of natural descent nor of human intent, nor of a husband's will, but born of God.
>
> John 1:12 (ACT)

And I did not understand that as a confirmed Christian I should grow in knowledge by daily Bible reading which is the source of spiritual food. For to be a growing Christian requires discipline and effort, not just wishing and good intentions. (My Daddy always liked to quote, "The way to hell is paved with good intentions.") Bible reading is a must for everyday's schedule; no one ever graduates from Bible study until he meets the Author face to face, for all Scripture is the inspired Word of God.

Confirmation is the moment when we publicly accept God's invitation to joy. It is a holy moment. It is our receiving the key to everlasting life from him who is waiting to hear from our own lips our request to come and live in us.

Our eternal life with God is a free gift, if we will receive it. Our goodness, kindness, generosity, and self-control are manifestations of the Holy Spirit living in us—not a way to earn God's love or forgiveness.

For it is by his grace you are saved, through trusting him; it is not your own doing. It is God's gift, not a reward for work done. There is nothing for anyone to boast of. For we are God's handiwork, created in Christ Jesus to devote ourselves to the good deeds for which God has designed us.

Ephesians 2:8–10 (NEB)

The growing practice of asking members of confirmation classes to pray a prayer of commitment several weeks before the official confirmation service makes the event more meaningful. The ritual then becomes a public recognition of a commitment already made in the heart. Confirmation should be thought of in the same way as marriage. Each of the couple pledges to the other long before they come to the altar to exchange their formal vows. The service is only the outward seal. Similarly, the confirmation service is the outward seal of an inner commitment.

When my cousins inquired if I had asked Jesus into my heart at my confirmation, all I could honestly say was "I'm a member of the church, I go to church every Sunday." I was uncomfortable and nervous. I wanted to get away, but we were in a canoe in the middle of the lake. So, as they sug gested, I prayed a prayer asking the Lord Jesus to come into my heart. Just the same, I remained ill at ease, though I sensed that somehow the prayer was important.

My cousins were, quite literally, the first people to talk to me personally about Jesus. I did not forget the prayer of commitment, but neither did I grow in faith. I did not tell anyone about the experience, neither my parents nor my minister nor my friends. I had no literature to read, no guides for using the Bible, and I remained a stunted, sleeping baby Christian.

It puzzles me at times that none of those Sundays singing in New York churches added a personal dimension to my religion. I was a performer at a ritual, intent on the professional demands of singing, intellectually stimulated and even deeply moved by many sermons, but I do not remember hearing from any pulpit the call for a personal commitment to Jesus Christ. Perhaps it was not in vogue at that time in the "big city" churches of New York. I will always be grateful, however, for the care that Cantor Joseph Wolfe took in explaining Jewish tradition to me and to his family for inviting me into their home so that I could participate in their sacred celebrations such as the Seder, Hanukkah, and Yom Kippur. Through them I learned to acknowledge aloud, in the family circle, the greatness, steadfastness, and mercy of God and to know that to declare obedience to him is a strengthening, a life-giving act.

Although I was raised in the Protestant tradition, I had never been taught the significance of the lives of those two great men, Martin Luther and John Wesley, so important in shaping church history. Martin Luther was an Augustinian monk baptized, confirmed, and ordained in the established church. He was a preacher and eminent professor of theology. He was faithful to the traditions of his beloved church, going so far as to practice such austerities as extreme fasting, flagellation, exposure to cold, in hope of drawing nearer to God. "I kept the rule so strictly that if ever a monk got to heaven by his sheer monkery, it was I," he wrote. "If I had kept on any longer, I should have killed myself with vigils, prayers, reading and other works." But he began to wrestle with the problem of man's relationship to God as exemplified by Romans 1:17:

For the gospel reveals how God puts men right with himself: it is through faith alone, from beginning to end. As the scripture says, "He who is put right with God through faith shall live." (TEV)

Finally, he understood that it is through faith alone that God justifies, or forgives, our sins. Through faith alone we can be brought into fellowship with the Lord. "Thereupon," Luther recorded, "I felt myself to be reborn and to have gone through open doors into paradise." It heartens me that the great hymns of this reformer are now sung by the same Roman Catholic Church from which he was forced to separate. Today many Lutheran ministers are lecturing in Catholic universities and Catholics are teaching in Lutheran schools, for under Christ we are all one.

John Wesley was an eighteenth-century Anglican preacher who came from England to America as a missionary to the Indians in Georgia. Like Luther, he was dedicated to his church. Although at first he was not an enthusiastic "born-again" Christian, he was later transformed into an instrument of God. This is how he described his conversion:

> In the evening, I went very unwillingly, to a Society in Aldersgate Street where one was reading Luther's preface to the Epistle of the Romans. About a quarter before nine, while he was describing the change which God works in the heart through faith in Christ, I felt my heart strangely warmed, I felt that I did trust in Christ, Christ alone for salvation, and, an assurance was given me that he had taken away my sins, even mine and saved me from the law of sin and death.

From that time on he preached faith and transformation—a person-to-person sharing of the experience of a Christ-filled life—to workers in the industrial cities as well as laborers in the countryside. The Evangelical Revival in which he was a major leader swept over all of England and was transported to America as well. It called for a return to personal faith. It not only affected the religious establishment, but also brought about profound social reform in the sphere of daily morals and manners, and political reform in the area of labor legislation. From it came the "Method" which is the personal sharing of what Jesus has done in a life. What a pity it was that no one tried the Method on me earlier in my life.

Being a Christian is to have strength, joy, peace, and radiance in the midst of daily problems, yet it is sometimes scary, for a Christian never knows where the next step will lead him. God says, take one step at the time and I will give the protection and guidance for the next step. God has not promised that the road will be smooth; there will be roots, stones, puddles, and potholes. He says, "Trust me and I will be a lamp unto your feet." At night after a fishing trip when we hiked back to camp through the woods, our lantern lighted only a small circle of light along the path so that we could see no more than one or two footsteps ahead. With the same faith a Christian is content to take just one or two steps at a time, knowing that God is our guiding light and will show us the next move.

An ethical, moral, trusting life is not enough. The Gospel commands: "Go and tell." Christians must learn to talk about the difference Jesus makes in their lives, earnestly, joyfully, easily, unembarrassedly, and with as much enthusiasm as they talk about their husbands, their children, their new house, or their golf game.

Pew Warmer

My marriage to Sonny did little more in terms of my religious experience than to shift the setting of my perfunctory worship. I was still a "pew warmer." There was no Lutheran Church in our area, and I felt then, as I do now, that it is usually better if families worship together. Since the Whitneys had always attended the Episcopal Church of the Advent in Westbury, we worshiped there. I did my duty, but that was limited to the formal aspects of attendance and support. I sang occasionally at our church and in others. Along with the other women of the congregation, I worked diligently on the annual fund-raising fair, gave to Episcopal charities, and enjoyed the social aspects of the church relationship.

When we were at Whitney Park in the Adirondacks, I attended church regularly and sang solos in the local church when the minister graciously invited me. Distant cousins of mine, Dr. and Mrs. Robert Searle, had a summer camp in the area. He was minister of the historic First Reformed Church in Albany and then of the Madison Avenue Presbyterian Church in New York City. During our summer months at Whitney Park we used to have what we called "Searle Sundays" at the Methodist Church at nearby Long Lake. Bob would preach the sermon, his daughter-in-law would play the organ, and I would sing the offertory solo.

In those days I also took my churchgoing habit with me when I traveled abroad. I attended services at St. Peter's, Eton Square, in London, the church where my father was baptized and sang in the choir. Sonny and I took communion from the Archbishop of Canterbury, Geoffrey Fisher, in Westminster Abbey during Derby Week, 1956. In Rome, Paris, the Low Countries, and in Central America, I worshiped in the historic cathedrals. How very proud I was of my churchiosity. But I was only a pagan with a little fringe on top for Sunday morning.

As a "frozen Christian" I prayed, or I thought I prayed. I made petitions to God in my head, mostly "shopping lists" of what I wanted to receive or to happen. Time and again I decided to read the Bible. My idea of reading the Scripture was to start with Genesis, chapter one, verse one, and move straight through to the final period in the Revelation of St. John. I read through the first few episodes of Genesis, then came to the "begats" and got "besunk"!

At that time the only translation I knew about was the King James Version, which was completed in 1611. Today there are many contemporary translations to help us grasp better the meaning and the message of the Word of God as it applies to our everyday lives. Still I admire the poetic beauty of the language in the King James Bible and I usually memorize from this version. To hear what Moses, Isaiah, Hosea, John, Matthew, Paul, and the other writers say, in words and images common to today's experience, is, however, of greatest importance in order to make the Word of God more accessible to new generations. It was an act of great foresight when the American Bible Society, one of my favorite organizations, published *Good News for Modern Man, The New Testament in Today's English Version.* It is translated from the original Greek, and it reads smoothly in words any of us can understand. It has now received the imprimatur of the Roman Catholic Church. The TEV is used around the world, especially for new readers. With its delightful line drawings it is far removed from the discouraging Bibles of my childhood.

There are many other good modern translations, too: Moffatt; J. B. Phillips; the Revised Standard Version; *The New English Bible; The Jerusalem Bible;* the new *A Contemporary Translation* published by the New York Bible Society.

Humanitarian

Before I became an aware Christian I contributed to benevolent causes as a humanist, an ethical person genuinely concerned about the physical and educational needs of persons. It was the proper thing for a "Mrs. Nicodemus." My giving was not hypocritical; it was merely incomplete. Almost unknowingly, I selected a few causes which increased God's kingdom. One of those was the Salvation Army, which I knew did a great work yet I didn't know exactly what. Like many people, I saw the Salvation Army as a tambourine-playing, drum-beating group in quaint uniforms standing on the street collecting money in a soup kettle to help the drunks in the Bowery. But its major commitment is much more. We—

I am now on the Salvation Army Board of Directors—have hospitals and homes for the sick, the indigent, and the aged; we care for unwed mothers, help unwanted children, alcoholics, drug addicts, prisoners, the crippled, and the retarded. We support playgrounds, recreation facilities, and social centers, and are active in seventy-four countries. In the U.S.A. each year nearly 22,000,000 meals are served by the Salvation Army to homeless people; 39,000 men and women are provided with work in 63 occupational centers; 219,000 prisoners receive Salvationist visitors; 5,000,000 people are assisted in emergency and disaster; 480,000 families receive help in time of need; 169,000 unemployed people are helped to find jobs; 1,100 patients are cared for in leprosaria; 160,000 in-patients and almost 1,000,000 out-patients are treated at the Army's hospitals; more than 7,000 missing persons are located and 3,500,000 persons visited in hospitals and other institutions. The purpose of the Salvation Army is to rehabilitate people physically, mentally, and emotionally and, at the same time, to give them spiritual strength. The latter is the most important, for to be healed for eternity is the greatest healing of all. Salvation Army lassies may not wear bonnets designed by Mr. John, but look deep into the eyes of any Salvationist and there you will see peace, joy, love, compassion, and a desire to help others, to share their Christian faith with all those who suffer pain, loneliness, grief, and emptiness. The Salvation Army is the organization most dear to me in the world. If I could work for and contribute to only one group, I would choose the Salvation Army, for it heals the whole person.

"A 'Crusade'! What's That?"

Time rocked along for Eleanor Searle Whitney Nicodemus, the good rich lady who went to Sunday services, sang a few solos, gave organs and steeples and lighting fixtures, and prayed for divine guidance without thinking about what she would do if God responded.

Then, in early June, 1957, an Old Westbury neighbor, Mrs. William C. Langley (formerly Jane Pickens of radio's famed Pickens' sisters) invited Sonny and me to attend a luncheon at her home. After luncheon an attractive tall gentleman was introduced by the hostess and asked to "say a few words." I paid little attention either to the introduction or to the name. But, as I politely listened, I was extremely impressed with the pertinence of his remarks to the problems of the world at that time.

We were planning a lawn party for a hundred and sixty of our friends on June 17, and Jane requested me to include the speaker and his wife. I also invited some of his friends who were with him. After all, they were in New York doing something religious and "Mrs. Nicodemus" thought it was nice to be gracious to the clergy. The couple's name was Graham —Billy and Ruth Graham. They said they would come if they could possibly arrange it. Soon after, I read in the newspaper about this Billy Graham. He was holding an "Evangelistic Crusade" at Madison Square Garden in Manhattan. I didn't know what to think because I really had no idea of what either a "crusade" or an "evangelist" was.

Religious vitality was never acceptable on Long Island's North Shore. My discovery that Mr. Graham was holding a "Crusade" gave me a mild jolt. "Well, Eleanor," I said to myself, "you must be more careful about your casual invitations." Later in the week when I received word that the Graham party would come, I wondered what I had let myself in for. "Oh dear," I said, beginning to sound like Alice in Wonderland, "what will my friends think? Who ever could imagine entertaining an *evangelist* who was holding a *crusade* in a Manhattan sports arena at proper Episcopal Whitney House!"

The Grahams came to the party with several of their associates. The day was hot; we lunched on the portico where cool breezes from the Atlantic Ocean on the south as well as from Long Island Sound on the north swept up the hill and across the lawns. After luncheon I asked Dr. Graham to "say a few words." He spoke briefly, but pointedly, to an audience which included Supreme Court Justice and Mrs. Stanley Reed, the Baron and Baroness Eugene de Rothschild, Mr. and Mrs. James H. Van Alen, and Mrs. Archibald Roosevelt. I find in some notes I made in my diary that Dr. Graham told us that "the greatest stumbling block to the Kingdom of God is pride —ego. The 'I' has to be crucified and the ego denied." He said that he knew some of the people who "came forward" at his Crusades were not sincere and did not grow in their knowledge and love of God, but that many did experience a real change, a "sweeping, wonderful, radical change that transformed their lives." I found myself genuinely interested and later, in private, asked Dr. Graham a few questions about his Crusades. He invited me to attend one some evening.

The following Sunday, June 23, Dr. Frederic Underwood, our rector at the Church of the Advent, asked me if Billy Graham had been a guest at my home the week before. I nodded affirmatively and prepared for what I fully expected would be a scolding for sponsoring an evangelist. I tried to think of a defense, something more profound than "I didn't know who he was." To my great relief, Dr. Underwood smiled. "That's marvelous," he said. "I hope you'll invite the Graham team again so that I can come and meet them."

In the church bulletin the next week, Dr. Underwood reported the Billy Graham visits to Mrs. Langley's and to Whitney House. The account continued: "We invite all to follow through with what Billy Graham has started. We will help you with reading and learning more of the Gospel of Christ. The only question still is, 'Will you, by an act of your

own will, make this decision and follow through with us?' "
He urged all parishioners to attend the Crusades and proposed a car pool to help with transportation.

"Well, Eleanor," I said in my newly formed habit of talking to myself about Billy Graham, "maybe you didn't do such
a silly thing after all. If Dr. Underwood approves, it must be
all right to have your name associated with an evangelist." I
am so grateful that Fred Underwood was our minister. Had
he been one of those clergymen who discourage church members from going to Graham Crusades, had he been glib about
evangelism or had he even lightly ridiculed my invitation to
the famous preacher, I might never have discovered the joy
into which I now invite others.

Dr. Underwood was an enormously sensitive and wise man.
He had many academic honors, and he was deeply interested
in the spiritual and civic needs of his community. Later he
would become my spiritual mentor, but at that time he was
only an ecclesiastical authority figure. In formal churches
which are part of a cultural milieu, the clergy are often social
arbitrators as much as pastors and shepherds. Because I was
still only a "pew warmer," a fainthearted "Mrs. Nicodemus,"
a social, superficial rector could have easily turned me away
from the spiritual rebirth and the evangelical zeal which now
fills my life. Had Dr. Underwood objected, I probably would
have felt guilty for inviting an evangelist to my home. To do
social penance, I might have sung two solos on two suc-
cessive Sundays—to be "nice."

"But, I'll Feel Like a Silly Goose"

I agreed to take part in the nightly car pool into Manhattan
only because it seemed like a generous gesture and because I
had the time as Sonny had had to go to California. Yet, I was
fascinated by the Crusade, partly, I think, because it was a
novel experience.

Since our groups were going regularly, we had seats in the Garden reserved each night, as did other churches. The seats were held until a half hour before the service started. If no one filled them, the space was opened to the long lines of people who were always waiting. I was overwhelmed by the soaring sound of the 3,000-voice choir, composed of members of participating churches. I listened attentively to Dr. Graham's sermons, finding them inspiring and applicable to the day. He always spoke about the relation of Christ and the Bible to everyday things, of asking God's guidance in every act and decision, of relating to the Lord as to a loving father.

I was also amazed by the tremendous crowds which came to hear the evangelist. The Crusade lasted for sixteen weeks at the "old" Madison Square Garden on Eighth Avenue, during which time 2,357,400 people—an all-time record—attended. On the closing night in September, 100,000 packed Yankee Stadium.

At the end of each service, Dr. Graham issued an invitation for persons who wanted to firm things up with God to come forward. Night after night, with some of that same uneasiness I felt when my cousins asked me to pray a prayer of commitment, I watched streams of people going forward. I was more mature and sophisticated than I had been as a teenager, and I thought I could deal with life as it came along. Smugly, I looked at the hundreds thronging out of the stands and making their way up to the platform, and thought, "Isn't that wonderful! They need it."

Yes, *they* need it; *they* need to find God, to become usable. They, not me, not Eleanor, not the kind, humanity-loving Mrs. Cornelius Vanderbilt Whitney. I was a fourth-generation Lutheran, a winter Presbyterian in Florida, I attended a Methodist college, sang in synagogues, Catholic churches, and a variety of Protestant churches, and I married an Episcopalian. Others needed to commit their lives to God. I was at the

Crusade to do a good work for the church because Dr. Underwood had encouraged me and because by now I was a friend of the Billy Graham team members and their families. I did not think there was any need for me to go forward.

Following Dr. Underwood's suggestion, I arranged for a hundred or so guests at another gathering to meet and hear Dr. Graham and members of his team at Whitney House. I served tea in mid-afternoon on the Spanish patio. A very cheerful Fred Underwood and his wife, Dorothy, were present, as were some young, attractive executives from Oklahoma who had flown to New York for business and to attend the Crusade.

The businessmen, Carl Anderson and Ralph Yinger, and their wives, told my guests about the difference Jesus Christ was making in their lives and in the lives of others in their country club set after they had gone forward at a Crusade in Oklahoma. I had never in my life heard anybody talk so personally about Christ over tea. Never! It was amazing. Laymen speaking of Jesus in the middle of the afternoon! That *was* new.

The young men and their wives were not embarrassed. They were enthusiastic, filled with life and high spirits. My concept of laymen who spoke of Jesus in a personal way was of dour, dowdy, dull, drab persons who looked as though they had been weaned on a dill pickle. I was like the child who saw a dole-faced mule and said, "You look so sad; you must be a Christian."

My appreciation for the religious consciousness and life style preached by Dr. Graham increased. I became fond of Ruth and Billy as individuals and of members of the Graham team: George Beverly Shea, Cliff Barrows, Charles Riggs, Fred Dienert, Grady Wilson, T. W. Wilson, Sherwood Wirt, George Wilson, Walter Smythe, and Bill Brown, and their wives and the others. I invited them to make our estate a place of relaxation and recreation. Their only free day was Monday, and they came frequently, bringing their children, for swimming, riding, golf, tennis, and picnics on the lawn.

Billy Graham has not sought fame, but because he feels compelled to announce God's "good news" to mankind, he is one of the most famous and admired and listened-to men in the world. Sought out by presidents and monarchs, Billy Graham never seeks followers for himself; he simply tells people how they can know Jesus personally by inviting the Holy Spirit, the third person of the Trinity, to dwell in them. This is what really happens and people are changed. Christ doesn't reform, he transforms.

> Be not conformed to this world: but be ye transformed. . . . Romans 12:2 (AV)

He and his team invite others to accept Christ as their own. He does not force or badger, for he knows that each person must firm up his own faith, not because Billy Graham wants it, but because God himself loves us and longs for us to love him.

Isn't that a staggering thought? God always seemed "way out there" and I thought that he couldn't be bothered about me. The essential message of the Bible is, God wants to forgive us our sins; he came to earth in the body of a man, Jesus, specifically to give himself in payment for our misdoings so that we could be justified on earth and live with him for eternity. Justification means "Just-as-if-I-had-never-sinned"—as when a loving father pays for the car his child wrecked or for the windowpane he broke. God gave his own Son so we could be reconciled to him. This is how much God loves each one of us. This is the invitation to joy he extends to us all.

As I went to the Crusade again and again, I began to realize that I, too, wanted to know God personally. I saw that my life lacked commitment to divine purpose; I felt spiritually adrift. My mind returned to the prayer I had said many years earlier

with my cousins and I knew that my Christian faith had
remained stunted, had not matured and grown. I no longer
wanted to stand proud and straight in the light of my own
good works. I was willing to be bent and bowed before God
so he would forgive me and lift me up to stand for him. I
wanted to pray "God be merciful to me a sinner."

Could I get up in front of my Old Westbury friends, walk
down the aisle, and stand in front of the platform at the close
of a Crusade service? My heart said yes; my mind had doubts.
"But I'll feel like a silly goose," I told myself. I was afraid
people would point their finger at me and call me a "holy
Joe." Or quip, "There goes Eleanor, we always knew she
could use some religion."

But I wanted to get my life straightened out with God. For
years I had been using God without ever giving him a chance
to use me.

Then one evening I drove alone into Manhattan to the
Crusade. It was the only time I went without friends, and it
was in the last weeks of the Crusade. I was again like Nicodemus, wanting to sneak in to see Jesus at night, unseen by
friends. I slipped into a seat and nervously listened to the
music and sermon. When the invitation came and people
moved forward, I did not budge. I knew approximately how
long Dr. Graham waited until beginning a prayer with those
who came. Eleanor argued with Eleanor about this "very
silly, very unnecessary" thing. Suddenly, I was out of my seat,
trying to be inconspicuous as I hurried up the flight of steps
from the reserved section through the long vaulted, smelly
corridor that led to the ramp and onto the floor of the Garden. I edged into the crowd just as Dr. Graham was starting
the prayer. He directed us in praying a prayer like "Dear God,
I know I am not perfect. I know I am far from what you
would like me to be. I am a sinner. And I thank you for
making it possible to be forgiven. Thank you Jesus for shed-
ding your blood for me. Come into my life and forgive my

past. I want your Holy Spirit to dwell forever in my heart. Make me the kind of person you want me to be. Use me for your glory. Amen."

Dr. Graham told us we would find counselors wearing badges standing next to us. The volunteers would help us sign commitment cards, show us what we should read in the Bible, and give us literature. I had wept softly during the prayer. Opening my mist-filled eyes, I saw Ruth Graham standing next to me—my counselor. She had seen me come onto the floor and had followed. My tears became a waterfall as I rested my head on Ruth's shoulder. They were warm tears, because the cold place I had locked away in my heart was warmed by the Holy Spirit. The timid chill which I had never been able to describe was gone. That chill, that emptiness, had been my unawareness of God.

New Beginnings

If anyone had asked me the next morning what difference that prayer would make in my life, I never could have explained it. Can a newborn baby say what he will be when he is grown? I knew that as a Christian I had waked up and that I had made a spiritual reaffirmation of faith. I had bridged the gap between my new faith and the vows I made when I was confirmed and the prayer I had prayed with my cousins. A person is not automatically a mature Christian the minute he asks God to forgive him and requests Christ to take control of his life. That is why the Graham Crusades, in any city or town, are always followed up by local volunteers and by mail contact with the Crusade association office. The "born again" Christian must learn to read and study the Bible, to pray, to find inspiring and informative material, to talk to others about faith, and to learn to share the glories of God's grace, the richness and joy Christ's indwelling brings.

But I did not dream of telling anyone what I had done, nor

did I think that anyone would ever find out. I thought I could continue to keep my faith to myself and have a secret love affair with God. You see, I still was not sure that it was "good taste" to come forward at an evangelistic crusade. This was part of my immaturity as a Christian. I was continuing as a "Mrs. Nicodemus"—phase two.

Nicodemus does not disappear from the Gospel of John after his nighttime visit to question Jesus. Near the end of chapter seven, he comes forward, cautioning his fellow officials, who are inclined to condemn the young Nazarene without trial, that they must judge him according to law and give him a trial. Nicodemus speaks a good, if limited, word— rather as I had done in sponsoring the Billy Graham visits to Old Westbury. The last mention of the prominent Jewish leader is in John 19:39, when he helps Joseph of Arimathea, who has received permission from Pontius Pilate to take Christ from the cross, prepare the body for burial. A wonderful gesture? Of course, but both Joseph and Nicodemus must carry out the burial in secret because they are afraid of the Jewish authorities.

Without knowing anything about Nicodemus, I expected to keep my religious reawakening to myself. Oh, there are so many, many "secret service Christians"—persons who want to keep their faith locked within themselves, or perhaps they long to tell but have not learned "how-to." But the church can be filled with spiritual life, fire, and joy only when Christians freely open their hearts and go forth and tell. Would the message of Jesus Christ have spread throughout the nations if the disciples had imitated Nicodemus' "secrecy"? Never. For inspiration and example of what happens when one lets God use him read the book of the Acts of the Apostles. Then read the many books written about or by modern Christians who have a new dimension in their own life and through whom God is working. These accounts read like a modern book of Acts.

Modeling Empress Josephine's diamond tiara from Van Cleef & Arpels, jewelers, and gown by Elizabeth Arden. Charity Ball.

Camping and cooking,
Whitney Park, Adirondacks.

Searle feeding porpoise, Marineland, Florida.

Playing Empress Josephine with Mr. John, the couturier-milliner, as Napoleon. Diamond and emerald tiara was Napoleon's gift to his second wife, Maria Louise, in 1811. Charity Ball.

Singing the National Anthem the night President Truman was nominated, 1948 Democratic Convention, Philadelphia, with Speaker of the House, Sam Rayburn.

Singing in the Chapel, Florida Southern College, Lakeland, Florida.

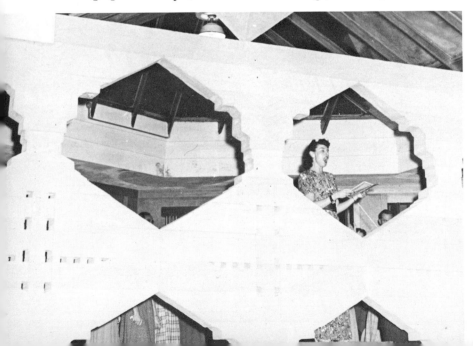

In Monument Valley with John ("Duke") Wayne.

Prince Aly Khan.

Clark Gable—two Buckeyes.

In one of the caves in which Dead Sea Scrolls were found.

Going down into new mine shaft in a mucking bucket. Hudson Bay Mining and Smelting Company, Flin Flon, Manitoba, Canada.

The "cup" which shepherds fill with water by lowering goatskins into a nearby well. When the "cup runneth over" the sheep can drink. Near Bethlehem.

Masai natives at Loitokitok, near Mt. Kilimanjaro, Africa.

Thirteen feet up on "California." Sahara Desert, Egypt.

Going down into the sacred kiva, or underground council chamber, with Hopi chieftain at Old Oraibi, Arizona.

With Dr. Billy Graham at opening of new building of American Bible Society in New York City.

Speaking at Ladies Prayer Breakfast in Washington, D. C.—with Mrs. Lyndon B. Johnson.

Something keeps us silent about our faith, warming pews, going through the motions of worship and never waking up mentally or spiritually and remaining incognito Christians. The clergy joins the "secret service," too, when they preach only about fund raising, buildings, construction, ethical do-goodism, and social action without challenging their congregations with a living Lord who wants to claim and transform them. Sometimes we are more anxious to gain church members than to get people on fire for Christ. We are like the grease factory which has no shipping department because it needs all the grease it makes to keep its own factory running.

Fortunately, my spiritual reawakening was not kept secret. Unbeknown to me, the Crusade officials sent a card to my minister, Dr. Underwood. This is a usual part of their follow-up program. Dr. Underwood was pleased and enormously helpful to me in the process of my maturing in faith. He never said, "Now, Eleanor, are you really sure about this experience? Don't you want to reconsider it? Why, you've always been a Christian. Your great-grandfather built a church in Ohio. You have uncles who were clergy. You and Sonny have always given generously here. Don't let this experience upset you."

Fred Underwood understood what had happened. He was overjoyed that some new spiritual zeal was present at the Church of the Advent, for I learned later that three of my close friends had also gone forward at Madison Square Garden to firm up their faith. With the encouragement of Dr. Underwood and the Graham team, we started a Bible study group. We invited Dr. Underwood occasionally to speak to us on a particular passage of Scripture, but mostly we dug out meanings ourselves, for we had found that it was embarrassing to ask elementary questions in front of learned professionals. We wanted to be as open and as free as possible to get over the surprise and timidity we initially felt as we confronted the Scriptures seriously for the first time. Often a Graham team member came to conduct a series of discussions. We studied one chapter a week, starting with the Gospel of John, reading, searching, and exchanging insights with one another. Having a teacher prevented our little group from merely sharing our ignorances. Our Bible study was aided by outlines mailed from the Graham organization. We returned our completed forms for checking and correction.

We strengthened our understanding by memorizing verses each week, always including the reference "head" and "tail" so we would know where to find them. For instance:

> John 3:16–17—For God so loved the world, that he gave his only begotten Son, that whosoever believeth in him should not perish, but have everlasting life. For God sent not his Son into the world to condemn the world; but that the world through him might be saved.—John 3:16–17 (AV)

It was all new to me—reading and studying the Bible, raising questions about the application of faith to daily living, and learning really to pray. We were encouraged to have a quiet time to be alone with God each day for study and prayer. I truly was a new person. How appropriate the words of II Corinthians 5:17, one of the first verses we memorized:

> Therefore if any man be in Christ, he is a new creature: old things are passed away; behold, all things are become new. (AV)

We also learned to pray with others. The first time I prayed aloud at the discussion groups, how nervous and self-conscious I was. And yet I had sung for years before the public. We learned that praying aloud even in our private meditations at home helped us to grow accustomed to hearing our own voices speak to God. It is amazing how disconcerting many of us find it, trying to address God in our very own words and sounds. We'd rather settle for prayers read in anonymous unison or let the ministers do the praying for us. Our group also encouraged prayer partners for daily shared prayers over the telephone.

One of the most memorable prayers we had at our class was at Thanksgiving time. One girl prayed, "Dear God, at this Thanksgiving time, I thank you for my Bible class. Amen." The girl next to her prayed, "Me, too, Lord. Amen." Those were real prayers.

We invited our friends to come to our study meetings. My, my, did we get some pained expressions. They could hardly believe their ears. And I never knew so many of the women in our community played golf or had their hair done on Thursday mornings. Naturally, we were laughed at, and called "the Angels" or "Cadillac Christians." Some said, "The girls are on a Bible binge." Still our group grew. Eventually it was divided, and divided again, and our lay movement on Long Island spread into many communities. Our members always travel a great deal and they start study groups wherever they are. I am sure that literally hundreds of Bible groups have been inspired because four women in Old Westbury decided to study the Good Book together after having made "secret" commitments at the Billy Graham Crusade.

Once the discussion group was off the ground, we were encouraged to take turns in leading it ourselves rather than depend on outside teachers. I knew the women so well, yet when my first turn as leader came, I felt frightened and deeply inadequate. My assignment was a chapter in the book of Acts. I wanted some new source material. Sonny and I had many Bibles, including an impressive two-volume set of the Bible twenty inches wide by thirty inches high, with exquisite etchings of biblical scenes, but they contained no explanations. I had bought a few commentaries, but the other women had them, too, and for my lesson I wanted to be able to share some new information. As our home library and the local public library were practically bare of explanatory books on the Bible, I set out for the New York Public Library on Fifth

Avenue, choosing a day when I could conveniently combine my research with an early evening reception off Park Avenue in the sixties.

I marched confidently between the two huge stone lions keeping watch outside the library, through the vast lobby, and upstairs to the reference library. But what should I ask for? I explained my problem and was provided with several enormous, dust-covered tomes which told me nothing about Acts except historical background. What I read was interesting, but I learned nothing about how to understand the meaning or apply it to modern life.

Slightly disappointed and weary from all my good intentions, I returned to the car, which I had left in the care of an elderly man who had agreed to drive me into the city. Somehow he had neglected to lock the door on the street side when he stopped for supper, and the small suitcase containing my change of clothes for the reception was missing. A large matrix emerald which had belonged to Evelyn Walsh McLean, the former owner of the Hope diamond and our neighbor in Washington, had also been stolen. I had to go to the party in my street clothes. That was not such a disappointment, but when the driver failed to return to take me home from the party, I became convinced that the devil was playing tricks on me to discourage my study of Biblical literature. Eventually, I called the police and we cruised around in a squad car until we found the car, the driver sound asleep behind the wheel. I decided right then that I would begin my own collection of reference materials and have a personal library of them on hand for myself and my friends.

Eleanor Searle Whitney Nicodemus was beginning to come out of hiding.

CHAPTER SIX

Valley of the Shadows

GOD'S PROVIDENCE was surely at work in bringing my faith
in him alive in the early summer of 1957, for shortly after I
firmed things up with God, I was forced to face a situation
which I could not have survived in any form resembling a
whole person if I had not been conscious of, and sustained
by, an abiding strength outside of myself. My husband made
it clear that he wanted a divorce. I know that I am only one
of a huge throng of men and women who have lived through
the breakup of a marriage and a home. But I also know that
the loneliness, the heartache, and the self-distrust they suffer
often lead them to seek distractions in bottles, pills, a psychiatrist's couch, or a series of empty dehumanizing alliances.
That I escaped these reactions was a work of the Lord.

I repeated over and over again verses I had memorized for
our Bible classes. One of these was:

> No temptation has come your way that is too hard for
> flesh and blood to bear. But God can be trusted not to allow
> you to suffer any temptation beyond your powers of endur-
> ance. He will see to it that every temptation has a way out,
> so that it will never be impossible for you to bear it.
>
> I Corinthians 10:13 (Phillips)

The verse cut into my heart and sustains me still.

Even now as I look back on my broken marriage, shadows of anger and despair blacken my heart. As I try to articulate this time of crisis in my life, I stir up memories and thoughts that I wish I did not have. I hope that in sharing them I will be able to convey a sense of the new power that has come to me as I have surrendered my anger and fear to God and he has transformed the energy of my hates and blame of self into joyful praise of his being.

I do not know precisely why my marriage went "on the rocks." When I married Sonny I knew that I was his third wife. But I loved him with all my heart, and I never had any reservations about my determination to make ours a lasting and happy life together. I vowed to do everything possible to maintain the mutual trust that is the necessary foundation of a fulfilling marriage. I think Sonny tried, too.

Although great wealth brings many pleasures and opportunities, I think it is hard for many wealthy men and women not to have a position that really needs them, that uses their God-given talents, giving their lives direction, challenging them to explore meanings and to mesh their lives with others in common endeavor. I have seen those who have not had to work, drift from one interest to another always superficially because commitment was not required, arrested for a brief time by a new car or a new boat or a new property or a new charity, new friends or even a new mate, until they strike out in search for a new distraction. They look upon everything in their lives as possessions and hope to find happiness or satisfaction from them, but emptiness, worthlessness, or inner loneliness is their constant reality.

Although I liked our many houses, I found always being on the move and making sure that the houses were cleaned, repaired, staffed, and ready to be visited extremely difficult. I seemed always to be packing or unpacking or both at once. I was never happy leaving my son. When we returned from a trip, he didn't say "Oh, Mummy, I'm so glad you're back," but "Mummy, Mummy, when are you going away again?" Even though I knew he had a loving and caring and capable governess, the pain of his words still makes me shrivel inside. I always wished Searle could have traveled with us, but so often that was not possible.

Marriage was sacred to me; I had said "until death do us part." So I prayed that God would keep my love for Sonny deep and full and flowing. Had love ceased perhaps it would have been easier for me. Had God allowed me to harden myself, the divorce might have caused me less suffering.

When Sonny left our home and did not come back, my world crumbled. My son was in the West on a ranch with friends, and we had already accepted an invitation from our Hopi friends to attend a special dance ceremony in Arizona given only once in ninety-five years. Feeling my life had to continue, I went. While there I was to discuss the details of the forthcoming performance of Indian dances at the New York Knickerbocker Ball. I did not want to let them down, since I had been trying for years to stimulate interest in the Indians among my friends in New York and hoped if they saw the lovely dances and crafts, the Indians' great worth and their plight would be better understood. Upon my return from the Hopi reservation I found a story of the Whitney divorce in the columns of almost every newspaper.

A Hectic Autumn

That autumn I stayed with the children in the Adirondacks later than usual and returned to Long Island to an extremely busy fall schedule. I took no action toward the divorce. The Bible study group was developing in Old Westbury, and I accepted more social responsibilities than I normally would have, partly to keep myself from brooding on my troubles.

I heard rumors that Sonny planned to seek a Nevada or

Idaho divorce and remarry. I did not believe he would or could so long as I was legally his wife.

But early in October I could no longer deceive myself. On October 3 I went to River House to change my clothes and found the door open. When I asked why my apartment was not locked as was customary, I discovered that all the locks had been changed and the locksmith had left it ajar.

That month was a nightmare. Still thinking I could distract myself by keeping busy, I modeled for the Blue Grass Ball to benefit the Travelers Aid Society, judged and presented awards for the Diamonds-International competition, met continually with the committee planning the Knickerbocker Ball, and worked on the United Nations Hospitality Committee, a group which welcomes and entertains diplomats and their families. My mother was able to come from Plymouth to stay with me and strengthen me, as my father had died a few years earlier. I don't know what I would have done without her wise and gentle advice. I never heard her say an unkind word about anyone in all her long, long life.

On October 21, Queen Elizabeth and Prince Philip visited the City of New York. I not only wanted to go to the luncheon, receptions, and ball, but I felt I should go to demonstrate if only to myself that life must go on.

During the last week of the month there was a testimonial dinner for Billy Graham, the opening of the Metropolitan Opera, and a small party of my own at Whitney House.

I hesitated in going to court, but finally, I had no other choice. It was nearly impossible to pay the household bills. To have moved out would have meant capitulation; I struggled on, conserving what funds I had and praying for strength.

It was November 19 that my attorneys filed suit in the New York State Supreme Court for separation and alimony. I was advised to charge abandonment without cause. About ten days later, Sonny filed for divorce in Nevada. My lawyers went to court again, obtaining a temporary injunction ordering Sonny to stop the divorce proceedings in order to show cause why he should not be permanently restrained from seeking a divorce anywhere but in New York State. Another part of the court action sequestered my husband's New York funds and property.

Flight

These court actions led to complicated repercussions.

The question of Searle's custody posed problems. It was decided that I must take him out of the state and live incognito until we could return. And so I fled with my son, informing only my mother, who remained at Whitney House.

I told Searle he might be gone some days. He was scheduled to play the piano in his school's Christmas program. When we left on that freezing night in December, he packed his dark suit because he hoped we would be home in time for the concert. My eyes flood with tears and my heart is filled with love and agony even now when I think of it.

I did not take my own car in case we were followed. A friend's butler rented me his automobile of exceedingly old vintage. He also loaned me his coat and hat. We drove away in the middle of a blizzard with absolutely slick tires and a steering shaft held together with wire and electrical tape. I was and still am grateful to that gentle butler who offered me his car with no questions asked.

Where would we go? I did not really know, but we did not go far that night. I kept hoping the foul weather would improve, but it didn't. We had to keep on the move every day, and so I headed south. The second night we spent at a small motel across the Delaware River from Newcastle, having slipped and slid the entire way.

I could never drive fast because of the condition of the car and the weather. During the trip I bought all new tires and we became expert tire changers. The weather was frightful the entire time. It took thirteen hours to cover one stretch of road that usually took three hours. And I had to make jokes of all the problems to keep my son from knowing how my heart was breaking.

It was necessary to telephone every day to find if it were wise to return. That chore was a nuisance as well as nerve-racking, since it was difficult to be near a telephone where I could speak in privacy. But we were not in a hurry. I decided the trip might as well be educational for Searle. I summoned as much joy and calmness as I could. I hope Searle never knew how much I wept after he was asleep at night. Only then could I stop pretending that we were on a fun trip and allow the reality of the situation to come into focus. We toured Annapolis, Washington, D.C., Mount Vernon, Richmond, Williamsburg, Jamestown, Yorktown, Monticello, Charlottesville.

Never, never will I erase the memory of our arrival in Washington. We got there on the very night I was supposed to arrive to spend the weekend as a guest of a dear friend of many years. She was giving a dinner before the opening of the ballet that evening. I drove aimlessly and tearfully around the city I knew so well, looking for an obscure place to stay. We could not go to the Shoreham or any other hotel where I was known. Perhaps by instinct, I found myself in Georgetown. It was just the hour when my friends were coming out of their homes in their furs on the way to the ballet gala. And there I was disguised in the butler's coat, his hat pulled down over my eyes, and forced to hide in a community of friends.

Most of the time I managed to be cheerful for Searle's sake. With a different reason for being there I might have actually enjoyed the historic tours in Virginia. Searle bought a sack of firecrackers—rare things in New York in those days—and some Confederate money in Richmond. In Williamsburg we attended a performance of Handel's *The Messiah* at William and Mary College. Searle and I were both fascinated with the Colonial and Revolutionary periods and later made a fine scrapbook out of the postcards and mementos we acquired.

We wandered through western Virginia for several days. Then about a week before Christmas I telephoned New York and learned that we could go home. I heard the good news just after Searle and I had finished a tour of Luray Caverns, north of Charlottesville in the Shenandoah Valley. My son was so fascinated with the stalactites and stalagmites and other crystalline formations that he wanted to go through a second time. We took the tour again. I enjoyed it myself that time, so happy was I to be coming out of my figurative cave. We took the Skyline Drive north and arrived home for Christmas, but unhappily not soon enough for my son to play in the school program.

The legal proceedings were in virtual stalemate during the first weeks of the New Year, 1958. Sonny had not appeared to answer the temporary injunction against divorce outside of New York. His assets in the state were still sequestered.

On January 24 Sonny married in Carson City, Nevada, shortly after he had been granted a divorce in that state. He was, however, still under injunction not to proceed with divorce outside of New York State. Upon hearing the news of the marriage, I felt disbelief, shock, heartbreak, anger, embarrassment, confusion, failure, and defeat—all those emotions mixed together. I prayed for strength as I had been praying all along. My prayers did not ask God to turn back the clock so that my problems would be divinely erased, for God is no "special order" department for the relief of pain. Often God doesn't remove the pain or problem, but he can strengthen our inner resources to cope with the situation. I prayed to believe, trust, and obey, to wait patiently for the Lord. This is what faith is, an exercise in trust, and it takes energy and determination to pray, "Not my will, Lord, but thy will be done in my life."

Again, I had no practical plans. My lawyers and the court took over. Litigation in the New York courts dragged on and on.

In May I began to hope that the legal proceedings would come to an end. But it was not until July that the New York State Supreme Court finally announced a settlement.

I signed the papers and ultimately sued for and obtained a divorce from Sonny.

Serendipity for Eleanor

Searle and I left Whitney House on the weekend before the Fourth of July. Happily, we had a new house to go to. When it became evident that I had to leave Whitney House, I started house-hunting on Long Island. I had a few requirements. The ideal property should be relatively near my son's school. It should have no long driveway to maintain, a garage within the building, and a playroom for young people. Finding a house with that combination of features was not easy. I visited over seventy-five and reviewed descriptions of many more possibilities, but none was suitable.

I was thoroughly exhausted and discouraged. Then a set of coincidences led me to the perfect house. Friends had kept mentioning a certain small property with a moderate-sized house not far from the school. I checked into it, only to discover that my own real estate agent had sold it to a new owner six months before. By chance, one of my attorneys who was also retained by the owner happened to mention to her that another of his clients was having great difficulty finding a house. Apparently she realized the houseless woman was Eleanor Whitney, because a few days later, she called my real estate agent and asked him to bring me to tea. I took one look at the house and knew it was the place I wanted.

The owner told me that years before she had had a great

tragedy. At the time of her grief a friend had lovingly helped her, and she wanted to repay the kindness by offering me her house in my time of trouble. I was overjoyed and humbled by her generous spirit, which she said was guided by a higher power. I hope I can make similar selfless sacrifices to help others.

With a few adjustments the house was ready for us at the end of June. Our moving—though hurried—was made easier by another act of imaginative friendship which I shall never forget. My friend Max Feld is the owner of a large painting and maintenance firm. He offered to come out to Long Island to give his opinion on the structural condition of the house, which he found sound. He insisted, however, that it was in need of paint. In one week his men painted it both inside and out as a housewarming gift from him and his wife. Never has such generosity been so unexpected and so appreciated.

Serendipity is a word coined by Horace Walpole in 1754. It is derived from the ancient name for Ceylon and takes its meaning from a tale called "The Three Princes of Serendip." According to legend, as the princes traveled far and wide they discovered by accident or awareness or sagacity treasures they were not in quest of. Now it signifies the faculty of making happy, unsought for, unexpected, and unmerited discoveries of value; it means turning failure or disappointment into usefulness in a different dimension. All through the bleak months of separation and divorce, I was the recipient of countless expressions of serendipity. And so I named the new home that was to shelter my new life "Serendipity."

How can I describe the feelings of emptiness, embarrassment, and shame that swept over me when I first found myself involved in divorce. For although I had asked God to forgive the mistakes I made in my marriage and my inadequacies and lack of wisdom, fear was like a leaden cannonball in my stomach, often causing active nausea. If I had failed where I

had tried so hard, what could I expect in the future when I
would be so totally alone. There was no end to my self-
flagellation. If only I had tried this or tried that. I knew I
had "hung in there" through difficult times and hoped with
every fiber of my being to be able to bring joy and security
into our marriage, but it was not enough.

I worried about meeting my friends. How would they greet
me? Would they take sides? I didn't know on whom to call.
Then I knew that God, the source of all serendipities, was
constantly by my side as more and more I surrendered my
will to him. And he blessed me with loyal friends. The mail
brought countless letters filled with warmth and affection.
Dr. Joseph Sittler, Jr. took time out from moving in Chicago
and wrote me of his and his wife Jeanne's deep concern and
to remind me of our lifelong friendship. Jane Barkley, widow
of the former Vice President, asked me to come to her in
Washington when I wanted a place to rest quietly.

I was particularly touched and comforted when so many
of the older generation made special gestures of friendship,
trying to lift my heavy heart with words of encouragement
and counsel.

Mrs. Charles Oliver Iselin, who died in 1970 at the age
of nearly one hundred and three, was a fairly near neighbor.
Like my mother-in-law, she was delicate and slender with a
heart of gold and a will of forged steel. Punctuating her remarks with thrusts of a gold-headed cane, she told me that
the divorce was unfortunate but it did not reflect on me. I
must not be crushed. I must hold my head high, and though
friends were shocked, she would help me in every way that
she could. She wanted me to come to her and visit with her
often.

Another older lady friend was spending the summer at
her home on eastern Long Island, but she came into New
York City and even though her apartment was closed, insisted that I come there to see her. We drank tea among

the shrouded furniture, the covered paintings, and rolled-up rugs, and she gave me advice, which I still follow, on how to live in society without a husband. She said never to refuse an invitation because I didn't have a husband to escort me. Usually a dinner partner was provided, or I could ask if it were convenient to bring one, or I could simply be an extra woman. Once I got over the shock, I would remember that many interesting and attractive women were widowed; many, for one reason or another, had never chosen to marry; many had husbands whose business caused them to travel a great deal; and I certainly knew first hand the lot of the doctor's wife.

I am still uneasy about walking into a party alone. But I am aware of the small, thoughtful gestures of really loving friends as they come forward to greet me, include me in a conversation, introduce me to others. Isn't it sad that many of us become so concerned with ourselves or with "the party" that we are not sensitive to the opportunity of reaching out with a needed loving comment or act. I found it strange, too, to go to the opera or a lecture or a concert with another woman or by myself. But I realized that if I didn't wish to be forgotten or filled with self-pity, I must be my own ticket-getter and transportation and go fearlessly and cheerfully into the day or the night.

Mrs. Marjorie Merriweather Post, Mme. Perle Mesta, and Mrs. Elizabeth Nightingale Graham (Elizabeth Arden) also shared their observations, experience, and advice on the life of a single woman in the modern social world. We went over many emotional, social, and financial facts I needed to be aware of. They provided straight talk on what I should and should not do, on where I should and should not go, and on how to avoid the men who meant to be kind, but were thinking only of themselves. Those women became like older sisters to me, and I shall never forget their kindness.

In late 1958 my son and I were settled in our new home.

He continued at his school, riding the school bus back and forth. No matter if I had been late at the opera or a dinner party the night before, we always had breakfast together. I felt I should give him as much of a family feeling as I could, and of course my joy in being with him was boundless. Two years later he left for boarding school in Connecticut, and my mornings were less bright. I was now utterly alone.

Because of my growing involvement in God's work, many requests came, asking me to speak for Rotary and Kiwanis clubs, churches, universities, women's groups, and it was gratifying that I could be so used. But that did not obscure the fact that I was dismal. How easily I could have burdened my friends with complaints, cried on the shoulder of my minister, or spent my days at a psychiatrist. Although all of these outlets sometimes help, they could not have dissolved my loneliness. I could have lost myself in alcohol or ended my pain by "having an accident." How many nights the contents of the sleeping pill bottle beckoned to me. But I knew that my son needed whatever sense of family I could give him, and I could not cause my mother to suffer. And so I repeated constantly to myself:

> Come unto me, all ye that labour and are heavy laden, and I will give you rest.
>
> Matthew 11:28 (AV)

> Whom the Lord loveth, he correcteth.
>
> Proverbs 3:12 (AV)

> I give you my own peace and my gift is nothing like the peace of this world. You must not be distressed and you must not be daunted.
>
> John 14:27 (PHILLIPS)

I took God at his word and appropriated his promises, and he never left me.

In mid-December I made one of my few return visits to

Whitney House. For two days, much of the remaining contents of the house was sold at public auction. Books, prints, and paintings went on the block the first day; furniture and oriental rugs on the second. I bought a few items that I wanted for utilitarian or sentimental reasons, but that was all that I could do. I found it hard to stay at the sale, to watch dispassionately as the paintings I had hung and the furniture I had placed and used were sold as cold business to the highest bidder.

But the auction really imprinted the facts on my mind: Whitney House as I had built it, lived in it, and loved it was gone. I was making a new life for myself, I had a new home— Serendipity. And I went back to my own hearthside, certainly scarred by the divorce experience, but still a woman alive. I had come through the fire with a stronger faith in God; I knew the truth of Jesus' words in the final verse of the Gospel of Matthew, "Lo, I am with you always."

CHAPTER SEVEN

Beginning a New Life

IT IS EXTREMELY INTERESTING TO ME to look back over the first few years of my new life after the divorce. I can now trace the patterns though I was certainly not aware that the experiences were coloring and designing my life. Sometimes I think of it as the "thawing" of a "frozen" Episcopalian. Certainly the vibrancy of my reawakened faith warmed more than the church pew. I saw with greater and greater clarity that participation in a beautiful, ancient ritual varied by good music and a distinguished sermon was not enough, that true churchgoing demanded more than donning especially fashionable clothes once a week and helping kindheartedly with good works on a few other days. But I did not merely thaw; I know that in some wonderful way I also grew.

At the beginning, though I was a rededicated Christian, I was a mighty silent one. I nurtured the joy of having Christ in my heart, I continued with my "quiet-time," careful daily Bible study, worship, prayers, and the Bible classes with my friends. Then gradually I felt a growing conviction that I must learn to share what Jesus had done in my life.

In retrospect I think it was also a sort of tunneling; guided by God's love, experience followed buttressing experience until a way was made to the light of understanding a more complete and useful Christian life. It seems as well to have been a time of coming into focus. I had prayed all my life, I had learned discipline and service through helping my father and in my singing career, and even running the Whitney houses. There had always been a song in my heart and I had always loved people. During this coming-together period all my past experience and training were to be bound together and made abundantly fruitful for my new mission of inviting others to a life of joy.

As my circle of Christian friends grew, I discovered that the world of Christian work and witness was fresh and exciting. I was fortunate to "wake up" at a time when laymen in many professions were speaking personally for the living God. The list of prominent Americans who are bold in their witness for Christ would fill books. There are government leaders on all levels; astronauts such as John Glenn, Frank Borman, and Buzz Aldren; actors such as Pat Boone, Roy Rogers, Dale Evans, and Dick Van Dyke; singers Andy Williams, Johnny Cash, Anita Bryant, Norma Zimmer, and Tiny Tim; Metropolitan Opera star Jerome Hines; sports greats Jerry Koosman, Rafer Johnson, Fran Tarkington, Bobbie Richardson, Bill Bradley, Bill Wade, and Bill Glass, who is now an evangelist, giving his entire time to working with young people; Charles Shultz who draws the "Peanuts" cartoons; Dr. Everett Koop, pediatric surgeon of Philadelphia, and other great doctors; many Miss America winners and student leaders. In the business world there are George Champion, former chairman of the board of the Chase Manhattan Bank, who in a way is responsible for my becoming a turned-on Christian, for he was chairman of the 1957 Billy Graham Crusade; F. Russell Esley, chairman of the board of U. S. Bank Notes; Walter Hoving, chairman of the board of Tiffany; J. C. Penney and Henderson Belk, department store owners; Maxey Jarman of GENESCO, Inc., which owns Bonwit Teller, Henri Bendel; Roger Hull, chairman of the board of MONY (Mutual of New York) ; Elmer Engstrom, chairman of the executive committee of RCA; Arthur de Moss, founder of National Liberty Assurance Company; Dave Swanson of Thomas' English Muffins; Wallace Johnson, co-chairman of the board, and William Walton, president, of Holiday Inns. And there are hundreds of others like you and me, whom God is using to spread his joy in their spheres of activity.

At the same time I became acquainted with many of the organizations that spearhead and continue to carry on the work of spreading God's word of love, reconciliation, and forgiveness. In 1958 the head of a large business enterprise invited me to a Presidential Prayer Breakfast in Washington. Prayer breakfasts for public leaders on municipal, state, and national levels—abroad as well as in the U.S.—were started by the International Christian Leadership, an organization founded over thirty years ago by Dr. Abraham Vereide, a "modern Viking" from Norway. These interfaith breakfasts are attended by citizens, often numbering in the thousands, who have concern for the community in which they live. They inspire the formation of smaller groups for weekly Bible study and for helping each citizen learn how better to appropriate God's promises in their business, civic, and home life. Prayer breakfasts for our country always remind me of God's response to King Solomon's prayer at the dedication of the first Temple in Jerusalem:

> . . . if my people who bear my name humble themselves, and pray and seek my presence and turn from their wicked ways, I myself will hear from heaven and forgive their sins and restore their land.
>
> II Chronicles 7:14 (JB)

Our nation was established on a belief in God. Even Benjamin Franklin, who was not known for advocating traditional piety, asked for a time of prayer during a difficult moment in the framing of the Constitution. My belief in the moral strength and worth of America was heavily underscored when I went to the 1958 Prayer Breakfast and saw so many leaders—senators, representatives, judges, civic and business leaders, and cabinet members assembled for spiritual inspiration and prayer. President Eisenhower told of his own personal relationship with Jesus Christ and the guidance God had given him throughout his life. Vice President Richard Nixon spoke of his reliance on prayer, and of his spiritual beliefs, as did many members of Congress.

I am enthusiastic about the Prayer Breakfast movement and the work ICL does throughout the world. Over the years I have been privileged to attend, address, and sing at many breakfasts in Washington, and at state capitals and in cities where they are held as Governor's or Mayor's Prayer Breakfasts. Many towns have special luncheons for the Governor's or Mayor's wife because there is no hall large enough to hold both the men and women who want to attend. Also, many women who have children of school age find it more convenient to be away from home at noon. I am always thrilled to see a room filled with top public officials, business executives, and influential women united in asking God's direction for their state and nation.

In the summer of 1959, Searle and I went to Colorado Springs, he to visit friends and I to attend workshops and classes at the headquarters of the Navigators at nearby Glen Eyre. The Navigators is a lay group begun in 1932 by Dawson Trotman. Its purpose is to teach servicemen, youths, and adults to let God control and navigate their lives. Their international organization today has a strong evangelical emphasis and is an effective training agency for lay witness.

While I was studying at Glen Eyre, I made my first attempt to tell another person what Christ had done in my life and to ask him if he, too, wanted to know God personally, to be committed to him. One free afternoon I was watching water skiing from the patio of the Broadmoor Hotel where I was staying. A girl fell into the water, and I moved over to the railing to see her relaunch herself. Two men were also watching the water sports and we started to talk. They asked me what I was doing in Colorado Springs. I explained I was taking training in Christian witnessing at Glen Eyre. One man excused himself promptly to "catch a plane," meaning, I suppose, he did not want to hear any of that "religious stuff." The other was genuinely interested. At resorts, a single woman learns to be prepared to hear almost any line from a man looking for companionship. But I believed him and invited him to go with me to a dinner at the Navigators that night. He was unable to do so but asked me to telephone him afterward so we could continue our conversation on the patio.

When I returned, I was told he was waiting for me in the bar. Well, I thought, Jesus turned water into wine at the wedding at Cana so I suppose I can witness in a bar. I saw him as I started into the lounge and decided he had too many friends with him for a meaningful talk. Yet I felt compelled to follow through with a person who seriously said he wanted to know more about God. I left a note in his box, suggesting he telephone me the next morning. He did and we talked several times that day and part of the next, when he had to leave for the airport.

I was extremely nervous, and, I'm afraid, not very adept in witnessing. We were sitting by the swimming pool most of the time and the splashes of divers and the play of children were distracting. To add to my uneasiness, the gentleman recorded our entire conversation on tape. I thought that to help anyone know God as I knew him I had to start with Genesis and recount the whole Bible through the last book, the Revelation of John. I told him the story of creation, the promise of God to Abraham, the Hebrews' years in Egypt, Moses, Joshua, the prophets, David, Solomon, the decline of the kingdoms of Judah and Israel, the birth of the Messiah, his ministry, crucifixion, and resurrection, the travels of Paul and the tribulations of the early church. My goal was to quote the passage in the third chapter of Revelation, the twentieth verse:

Listen! I stand at the door and knock; if anyone hears my voice and opens the door, I will come into his house and eat with him, and he will eat with me.

(TEV)

I wanted to say there are three responses we can make when Jesus knocks: We can keep quiet and hope he goes away, we can go to the door and tell him to leave, or we can open the door and invite him in. I kept avoiding this explanation because the next step was to ask this comparative stranger to let God take control of his life right then, to surrender his will through faith, giving all his burdens to God to handle as he saw fit. I was really struggling to break through my own spiritual barrier. It was not until the second morning that I had the courage to challenge him. I clearly remember that the Will Rogers Chimes high on the mountain above had just finished sounding the hour. I asked my new friend to give his life to God, and he prayed his prayer of commitment with me. It was as much of a new frontier for me as it was for him.

Later when my son joined us, he turned on the tape recorder and all three of us heard his prayer. I was overjoyed, realizing I could now explain to another how to receive Christ into his life, for I had wanted that ability for a long time but had not known how to share my faith. Apparently that tape has been played for others, for I have received letters from numerous people, saying they had been helped by it.

I too was helped by that experience in Colorado Springs. I learned that you need not tell the whole Bible story to invite others into God's joy. Nor do you need to be a theologian. What is needed is a personal knowledge of God which can shine in all relationships and enough familiarity with the Bible to know where to open it and allow God to speak. For it is the Holy Spirit that changes the life, not the spiritual guide.

When someone evidences an interest in finding deeper meaning in life, feels guilty about his past, wants forgiveness, peace, and joy, or wants to know about eternity, we can explain God's plan for mankind. His love and forgiveness and reconciliation are available for the taking. Intellectual expertise is not necessary.

> For the message about Christ's death on the cross is nonsense to those who are being lost; but for us who are being saved, it is God's power. For the scripture says, "I will destroy the wisdom of the wise, I will set aside the understanding of the scholars." So then, where does that leave the wise men? Or the scholars? Or the skillful debaters of this world? God has shown that this world's wisdom is foolishness! For God in his wisdom made it impossible for men to know him by means of their own wisdom. Instead, God decided to save those who believe, by means of the "foolish" message we preach. Jews want miracles for proof, and Greeks look for wisdom. As for us, we proclaim Christ on the cross, a message that is offensive to the Jews and nonsense to the Gentiles; but for those whom God has called, both Jews and Gentiles, this message is Christ, who is the power of God and the wisdom of God. For what seems to be God's foolishness is wiser than men's wisdom, and what seems to be God's weakness is stronger than men's strength.
>
> I Corinthians 1:18-25 (TEV)

It's so simple it sounds foolish. Jesus said I'm knocking and waiting at the door of everyone's heart. When you hear me and invite me, I will come and live in you with the Holy Spirit and change your life.

A prayer of commitment is the beginning of a new relationship with God. He knows the attitude of the heart, and so the words are not of primary importance. One might pray a prayer such as this:

Dear God, I know I'm not perfect. Forgive my sins. I'm inviting you to come and live in me and make me the kind of person you know I can be. Lord Jesus, thank you for forgiving my sins. Use me in a new way in your church, my business or school, and my family. I'm giving me to you.

When you talk to God in a similar manner and invite Christ into your life by this act of faith, many things happen, among them:

Christ by the Holy Spirit will actually dwell in your life . . .

For this is God's plan: to make known his secret to his people, this rich and glorious secret which he has for all peoples. And the secret is this: Christ is in you, which means that you will share the glory of God.

Colossians 1:27 (TEV)

Your sins are forgiven and God will never remember them . . .

If we say that we have no sin, we are only fooling ourselves and refusing to accept the truth. But if we confess our sins to him, he can be depended on to forgive us our sins and to cleanse us from every wrong. And it is perfectly proper for God to do this for us because Christ died to wash away our sins.

I John 1:8-10 (*Living Letters*)

You become a child of God . . .

Some, however, did receive him and believed in him; so he gave them the right to become God's children. They did not become God's children by natural means, by being born as the children of a human father; God himself was their Father.

John 1:12-13 (TEV)

You are assured of Eternal Life with God . . .

He who believes in the Son of God has this testimony
in his own heart, but he who disbelieves God, makes him
out to be a liar, by refusing to accept God's own witness to
his Son. The witness is this: that God has given us eternal
life, and that this life is found in his Son. He who possesses
the Son has life indeed; he who does not possess the Son
of God has not that life. This letter is to assure you that
you have eternal life. It is addressed to those who give their
allegiance to the Son of God.

I John 5:10-13 (NEB)

*You are a new creature willing to have your life controlled
by God—he will show you his purpose for your life . . .*

I have come in order that they might have life, life in all
its fullness.

John 10:10b (TEV)

The following autumn I made my first public witness for
Christ. The International Christian Leadership was holding
a conference in Bermuda. Mother, who was then visiting me,
suggested that she, Eugenie Trumauer—for many years my
personal maid and dear companion—and I combine a vacation with the conference. The day we arrived Dr. Abraham
Vereide, the president of ICL, asked me if I would sing at
several of the services and tell my story at a luncheon. "What
do you mean, tell my story?" I asked him. He explained he
meant the story of the time God and I got our relationship
straight—God as God and Eleanor as his servant. I protested,
"There's not that much to tell. I was just a Lutheran girl
from Ohio, who had married the man I loved, who had gone
forward at a Billy Graham Crusade, and now had started to
study the Bible, had some heartbreaks, am trying to be
a witness for Christ." "Tell just that," answered Dr. Vereide.

I stayed up late into the night, writing and rewriting what
I planned to say in the ten minutes I was allotted. Nothing I

wrote sounded very profound or moving. So as Dr. Vereide suggested, I just told my story, stressing the fact that having a "religious background" is not enough to make one a disciple of Christ. It was the first time I had ever told "my story" aloud. My mother was there and my talk about my new awareness of God's love in my life strengthened the spiritual ties between us. It was not until then that I came to realize what a deeply spiritual person she was and had always been. Previously we had never discussed the matter of personal faith, but from then on we prayed together many, many times. She never knew the place nor the hour she became a "believing Christian," but she was certain she had made a full commitment. We rededicated our lives together, reaffirming our wish to let God use us completely. We trusted in God and thanked him for making our bodies his home, knowing that he is faithful to his promise.

Fisherman for Christ

I was surprised by the response to my talk. Several of the conferees asked me to speak at other meetings in their homes and churches in the States. At first I accepted only invitations to speak for groups on Long Island. Dr. Underwood often came and I took joy in referring to him as my "spiritual godfather." He once told me he wished that his seminary had taught evangelism and how to lead parishioners in a prayer of commitment and had encouraged witnessing. For you see, an evangelist is someone who tells or proclaims the good news of God's love and redemption and witnessing is simply one forgiven sinner sharing what has happened in his life with someone else and explaining how he too can have inner joy. Like a witness in a courtroom he tells what he has experienced, what he knows to be true.

Dr. Theodore Elsner of Calvary Memorial Church in Philadelphia was the first minister to invite me to speak in his pulpit. How I labored over that talk and how my knees quaked when I stood up to address the congregation!

I have now spoken in over 350 churches of all denominations at morning or evening services and my knees still quake. I know that all ministers do not take kindly to a woman lay evangelist standing in their pulpits. In one Midwestern congregation the concluding benediction was hastily pronounced before I began my talk, lest I intrude on the ritual. At another church I was asked to address the congregation from a place between the pulpit and the lectern. It did not prove to be a good location because no one could hear me. At last an older man spoke up. "If we are going to trust Mrs. Whitney with God's word, I think we should trust her with our furniture as well," said he, pointing dramatically to the pulpit. Some ministers, however, were more open to risking their dignity. One Episcopal priest introduced me in this way: ". . . and she's right here sitting in the bishop's chair, because this morning she is going to bring us the word of God, she is going to talk to us about our savior, Jesus."

I learned early in my role as "fisherman for Christ" that I must always continue my own study of the Bible and broaden my own understanding of faith by reading and listening to what the more knowledgeable had to say at conferences and in classrooms.

Early in the 1960s I attended summer sessions at Campus Crusade for Christ, International. For five summers I have attended their courses in In-Depth Bible Study and have taken training in how to present the promises of God in a scriptural, natural, unembarrassed manner.

Campus Crusade's international headquarters are at Arrowhead Springs, San Bernadino, California. The building was once a resort hotel, standing over natural hot springs. Long ago Indians came to the springs to be purified and rehabilitated; tribal warfare was tabooed there. On the side of the mountain, towering over the water, is an abstract configuration made by unusual plant growth which resembles an arrowhead pointing down to the springs, but some people think the configuration looks like the figure of Christ with outstretched arms. After World War II the hotel stood empty for several years before Campus Crusade purchased it. Each year the facilities are used to train a staff which numbers over two thousand and a volunteer corps of tens of thousands.

I am now an associate staff member of Campus Crusade. Founded in 1951 by businessman William Bright and his wife Vonette on the campus of the University of California at Los Angeles, it now has branches in more than 250 colleges and universities in the United States and in forty-five countries. Campus Crusade places a strong emphasis on the great historic doctrines of the Christian faith, personal evangelism, and Christian discipleship. Its work is divided into five major areas of endeavor. College and university campuses still receive its principal thrust. A branch for military personnel operates for the benefit of servicemen and their wives at home and abroad. A third popular program is Athletes for Action, whose members often give exhibition matches and then witness to whole arenas of sports fans during the intermissions. There is also a high school division of Campus Crusade, for today young people are reaching out for answers to the meaning of life well before they are in college. A fifth branch is for laymen within the organized church. It encourages a zealous, interdenominational ministry to groups and individuals and emphasizes the importance of the local church. Thousands of students and adults are active members of local churches as a result of this work.

Many denominations are becoming enthusiastic about the work of Campus Crusade, offering them strong support. In 1970 the Episcopal Bishops in the Minneapolis, Minnesota, area sponsored a Leadership Institute for Evangelism (LIFE) in which thirty-four churches representing eleven denominations, as well as Catholic parishes, participated. I was there speaking for ten days before the Institute. Over thirteen hundred church members took the training course and returned to their church communities with a new vibrancy and ability to communicate God's word.

The entire ministry of Campus Crusade for Christ is made financially possible by concerned Christians. Each staff member is responsible for his own support and, through his local church and interested individuals, must raise his designated salary prior to his assignment. This is the usual procedure for most other para-ecclesiastical groups devoted to sharing the truths of God.

There are many other dynamic interdenominational organizations for adults. Among those in which I have become interested are Christian Women's Clubs (CWC), Christian Business and Professional Women's Clubs (CBPWC), Christian Business Men's Clubs (CBMC), and Faith at Work. The work of the Wycliffe Bible Translators has particularly far-reaching impact. Members of this group live with remote tribes, learn the local language, and create for them a phonetic alphabet. They are then able to make a written translation of the Scripture and use it to teach the tribespeople to read and write in their own tongue.

New Vistas

The deepening of my understanding of the ways of God and man were greatly enhanced by travel in foreign lands. This was now possible for me as my son was in boarding school and I had no husband and my household duties were slight. I wanted to see new continents and explore places I had only skimmed over on previous trips. My luggage may have looked the same—perhaps more battered—but my travel was different from that of my married years. I did go to the wedding of Britain's Princess Margaret Rose, but increasingly I sought to experience countries and cultures from the point of view of everyday life and to see how God was working there. I visited missions, leprosariums, and retreat centers rather than couturiers, and talked more about faith than about horse races.

I have visited Nepal, India, Iran, Iraq, Syria, Jordan, Egypt, Saudi Arabia, Lebanon, Israel, Turkey, Greece, Yugoslavia, and many other parts of Africa. And I rediscovered much of western Europe, especially Rome and Scandinavia.

Sometimes it was lonely, frightening, and forlorn to travel around the world by oneself. Often I really longed for home and for familiar faces. Sometimes I questioned what I was doing by myself in a foreign, often remote country. Then my faith in Jesus gave me courage and, with openness toward unfamiliar people and places, I was led on many occasions to interesting new experiences.

In 1962 Mr. and Mrs. Donald Kendall—he is president of Pepsi-Cola International—invited me to join them on a trip to Africa. When our several weeks of traveling around the continent ended, the Kendalls went to Rome and I remained in Rhodesia as I had planned. The first evening I found myself having dinner alone in the large dining room of my hotel. There was an excellent orchestra, and quiet dancing. I was a bit lonely. My heart sank. No one I knew was within thousands of miles! While waiting for the meal to be served, I took a small Bible out of my purse and began reading. It became obvious that three men at the table nearby were discussing me. Finally, one came over to my table, politely introduced himself, and said, "We've been debating whether or not you are reading the Bible." He thought it remarkable that anyone would do such a thing in a public restaurant. We had a pleasant conversation. The men were attending a conference at the hotel, and later they introduced me to Commander Harold Grenfell, for whom they worked, and to Mrs. Grenfell. The next day Mrs. Grenfell invited me to luncheon and then to join her and her husband on an inspection tour of their copper mining operation in the Transvaal. Having gone into many mines, including Sonny's Hudson Bay Mining and Smelting Company in Flin Flon, Manitoba—I even went down standing in the muddy, swinging mucking bucket used to open new mine shafts—I was delighted to have a chance to observe different mining techniques. At this mine there are eighteen miles of tunnels, some at a depth of 529 feet, from which copper-bearing rock is extracted. It is sent up to the surface where it passes through an electronically controlled crushing and flotation mill which separates the metal from the stone. Finally, it is purified and smelted. It takes at least one-half a ton of unprocessed ore to yield one ingot of pure copper weighing twelve and one-half pounds.

The Grenfell home was on a mountainside with a magnificent view overlooking the mine and smelter and onto the plains and the veldt. Over three thousand persons work the mines, and housing, schools, hospitals, and recreational facilities are provided for them by the company.

During our visit to the mines, the Grenfells and I became close friends, and they asked me if I would extend my stay and go with them to their jungle ranch. The following week was one of the most exotic and delightful I have ever experienced. They stayed in their ranch house, and I lived in a small, round thatched hut called a rondovel. Often we cooked our meals out of doors, sizzling the meat on an old cultivator disc thirty inches in diameter, which, when propped up on a tripod, made a fine frying pan.

Animals of all kinds roamed their land. Some were so tame they could be fed by hand. There was an affectionate baboon, Jack, who plucked the hairs of my arm to get my attention, and six baby cheetahs who had lost their mother and had to be fed nine times a day with cow's milk and cod liver oil from babies' bottles. One moonlit evening I was sitting alone by my rondovel in the bush not too far from the river, listening to the animals, when the tame eland nearly as large as a horse wandered out of the dark and licked my hand, asking to have his ears scratched. He was called M-mpauff, which is Swahili for eland. Nuzzling my hand to make me continue tickling his ears, he put his head in my lap, and I lay my head between his horns, resting it on the back of his soft, silvery gray neck. Later, I wondered how I could have been so trusting. One startled jerk of his head and his long, straight, sword-sharp horns would have severed my jugular vein.

Other wild animals were less easily observed, but all night long I could hear them roaring and growling, howling and trumpeting, as they sniffed and prowled around my hut. There were dik-diks, baboons, impalas, elephants, giraffes, wildebeest, zebras, and as it was a cattle ranch, cows and calfs, bawling because they had been separated.

The birds were marvelous, too. There were red-eyed turtle doves, brilliant turquoise kingfishers, ostriches, widow birds with sweeping black tails, purple-headed Cape Paradise fly-catchers with long orange tails, and the hornbill which makes an extraordinary nest of twigs in a dead tree. When it is finished the male hornbill covers the nest and the female and the eggs with mud, leaving only a small hole through which she can be fed.

There were scorpions and crocodiles and flying foxes and snakes, the most impressive of which is the black Ancheta cobra which has a hood ten inches wide. I can still hardly believe that this friendship and enchanting experience came to me simply because I was reading my Bible in a hotel dining room.

Zanzibar

I met Varas Kassam, the leader of the Isma'ili Muslim religion on the island of Zanzibar, when, because I had only a light suitcase, I offered him my remaining baggage allotment at the Dar-es-Salaam airport. He and his wife invited me to stay in their home with his family on the fragrant "Clove Island." That visit extended to three weeks! Through them I experienced intimately the daily practice of the Islamic faith.

My previous knowledge of Islam was based on a purely social friendship with the Aga Khan, head of all Isma'ilis, and his son, Prince Aly Khan. That was during my "frozen" religious period, and my interest was historical rather than spiritual. Aly Khan asked Sonny and me to go with him on one of his official visits to the Isma'ili centers in India and in Africa, and I regret now that we did not go. Muslims, the adherents of Islam—which means "submitting"—are not properly called "Mohammedans," for they do not worship Mohammed as divine, but rather as a prophet, the human vehicle for God's final and eternal revelation to mankind. That revelation has been preserved, as Mohammed recited it, in the Koran, Islam's sacred book. Its opening phrase is often repeated: "In the name of God, the Merciful, the Compassionate." The two basic tenets of the faith are: "There is but one God and Mohammed is his Prophet."

Islam's spiritual foundations are found in the figures of Abraham and Ishmael of the Old Testament; it accepts much of that Scripture. It also uses some of the New Testament, but it emphatically rejects the teaching that Jesus was the son of God. Tension between Jews and Arabs are recorded in the Genesis story of the jealousy between Sarah, the mother of Isaac, and Hagar, the mother of Ishmael. It has been increased by the fact that Judaism, Christianity, and Islam share many of the same sacred areas.

How I wish that all people would try to overcome religious disagreements which lead to persecution and warfare. I have often gone to mosques in countries where women are allowed to worship in them, and have prayed to Jesus Christ, prostrated, in the Muslim attitude, on my face with my head pointed toward Mecca, the holy city of the Muslims. When I was staying at the Kassam home I slept in the same room as his daughter-in-law. When the dawn call to prayer aroused me, I would slip out of bed and, kneeling beside her, pray my thanks to God and Jesus.

My visit in their home coincided with the last days of the month-long Ramadan fast. During this period of discipline and purification the Muslims take no food or liquid—they do not even swallow their own spittle—from sunup to sundown. Ramadan is concluded by several days of festival and thanksgiving called Eide Mabarek, a period somewhat similar to our Christmas and New Year. The Kassams were gracious and included me in their holiday festivity. There were feasts and prayers, giving of gifts, parades, bands, flowers, and crowds in the streets. I saw the robed sheiks with their jeweled, curved scimitars thrust in their belts on their way to the Sultan's reception for prominent men—no women are ever invited. There were special programs with music, and I was asked to sing at one. A most amusing thing happened. After the scheduled performance of Arabian and Indian music, which uses a quarter-tone scale and is accompanied by finger bells and triangles, I sang "Strange Music" from *Song of Norway* a cappella. I have never heard an audience snicker, giggle, and laugh so much, but I continued singing. The master of ceremonies finally came through the curtains and motioned to the audience to be quiet. They simply had never heard Western music performed; to them it seemed very "strange music" indeed.

In the libraries and parks, at a meeting of the Girl Guides, and in the Kassam home I had many opportunities to talk about religion with young people especially. Many Muslims are often more familiar with the Bible than some Christians, and they asked if, when Jesus spoke of "another Comforter" in John 14:16, he meant Mohammed. I pointed out that the passage that follows—John 14:26—says the "Comforter" is the Holy Spirit who comes to dwell in us. Many of the young people showed great interest, and we had many Bible discussions.

While I was in Zanzibar, I visited the house where the body of the great missionary, David Livingstone, had lain, awaiting the ship to return it to England after natives had borne it from inland Africa where, as he requested, they had buried his heart at the foot of a great tree. I thought of ministers and mission evangelists who sometimes become discouraged with the results of their work. They should remember the minister who felt that through him only one person had come to know God, but that person was David Livingstone. Livingstone crisscrossed Africa, bringing for the first time to thousands of natives the reality of Jesus Christ.

I went to the United States satellite tracking station on Zanzibar and heard John Glenn report from Friendship 7 as he orbited the earth. On the monitors we could see the regular beat of his heart. How fantastic it all was! I was very proud of our nation's achievement.

In Africa I made a point of visiting many missions, leper colonies, Christian schools, seminaries, and churches. I was asked to speak at some of them. At the Dorothea Mission in Pretoria, South Africa, I was thrilled to find so many Africans coming for instruction in evangelism, among them a daughter of the chief of Swaziland. In Kenya I visited the second largest mission in the world, Kijabe, in the Rift Valley. The cornerstone of the main building had been laid by President Theodore Roosevelt. My friends, Herbert and Mildred Downing from New Concord, Ohio, run the mission. The dinner I ate was cooked on a stove and the dishes washed in a sink given by the parents of John Glenn, whom I had visited in their home in New Concord several years before and the three of us had prayed together in their living room.

I also made a wildlife photographic safari to the slopes of Mt. Kilimanjaro in the heart of the Masai country. The

Masai are seven feet tall and live in huts called *kigige* made of little sticks and plastered with cow dung. They are only four feet high. I was hospitably invited to crawl into one and share with the owners the mixture of fresh cow blood and cow milk, which is drunk from a gourd on ceremonial occasions. The following summer my son was in the same area, attending the Outward Bound Mountain School of Kenya. Although only seventeen years old, he completed the training course during which he slept alone overnight in the lion-infested bush with only two matches to build a fire to cook his food. He also climbed to the summit of snow-covered Kilimanjaro.

Egypt

Egypt is another land in which I have traveled extensively. I was there in the days when tourists were still allowed to climb the great pyramids. I managed to get myself to the top of the largest—Cheop's ancient tomb—pulling myself up from one huge hip-high stone to the next. As I surveyed the vast pyramid-studded desert, I began to think of the religion that had inspired these monuments to death, and I thanked God for having sent, three thousand years after they were built, a savior who is all simplicity and humility, and who is the resurrection and the life.

Whenever I am in the vicinity of Cairo, I hire a camel driver and a camel, which I now partly own, called California. California is a beautiful, majestic beast. He got his name when he was chosen by Cecil B. DeMille to be the lead camel in the epic film, *The Ten Commandments*. Often I go into the desert for the whole day, sitting thirteen feet high in the saddle, right leg curled around the pommel, and right foot hitting his neck as I give the vocal command *Har-r-jah* and he breaks into a run. One hand grasps the single nose rope by which the camel is controlled. We carry our lunches in huge brightly decorated saddlebags, sandwiches and fruit for us and alfalfa and sweet grass for California. The sure-footed lope of a camel has a rhythm like waves at the edge of the sea. Now that I am accustomed to it, I find riding extremely comfortable and, at a fast pace, exhilarating. When we stop for lunch we take off California's saddle and saddlebags and let him roll in the hot, dry sand. He loves to scoop it all over his body with his huge padded feet. I especially like to ride my camel across the silent sand in the cool clear moonlight, protected from the cold wind by a caftan and a kaffiyeh, or scarf, wrapped Arab fashion around my head so that everything but my eyes are covered. The stars seem close enough to pluck, and no matter how far away we are, the pyramids always loom black against the sky.

While in Egypt one of my most unusual experiences was attending the Billy Graham Crusade in Cairo. It took place in a tent set up on the grounds of the American University. I left the hotel early because I knew that there would be a crowd, but when I arrived I found that the gates of the university were already closed and great crowds were waiting outside. Word of the Crusade had traveled not only through Cairo and its environs, but into the far reaches of the delta and the desert and to the villages many miles up the Nile. Egyptians had journeyed—some for days—by foot, boat, and camel to hear the prophetic word of God proclaimed. The multitude pressing to get in was so great that the Crusade area had to be doubled and tripled. The sides of the tent, made up of ten-by-twelve-foot panels of fine white cotton laced together and appliqued in brilliant colored scrolls, were rolled up, opening the tent to the expectant throng. More powerful loudspeakers were installed. So many people carried tape recorders to the service that fuses blew and more generators had to be brought in.

Fortunately, as I had planned, I met Crusade team members at the gates and was able to stand with them behind the platform. It was extremely interesting to hear Dr. Graham's message translated into Arabic by an Egyptian Christian, a leading surgeon in Cairo. The response of the audience was remarkably enthusiastic.

The Holy Land

Of all the places I have been, of all the inspirational experiences I have shared in the nations of earth, the area that excites me most and draws me back again and again is the Holy Land—that part of the Middle East where the Old Testament patriarchs, prophets, and kings dwelt, where Jesus lived, died, and was resurrected, and where St. Paul began his ministry.

The Holy Land is made up of Syrian, Jordanian, and Israeli national territories. Because it lies in the path of the movement of civilizations from east to west and from west to east, it has always been involved in international strife. Great contrast in the quality of land—some arable, some grazeable, much desolate—stimulates internal tension as does the fact that it is a land holy to three religions: Judaism, Christianity, and Islam.

It is a beautiful and fascinating land, but the reason I am so fond of it is that being there has helped me to understand the Bible better. To see the configuration of the hills, the forbidding rock formations much larger but like the Badlands of South Dakota, the color of the earth, the great fertile plains, the lapping waters of the Sea of Galilee, gives me a clearer vision of biblical events. I have seen the devastation of Jericho; oasis wells similar to the ones where Rebecca gave water to Abraham's servant and his camel, and Jacob watered Rachel's flocks; the mountains from which Moses could see the promised land; the ruins of luxury-loving Roman Tiberias; the ravaged wilderness of Judah where Jesus fasted and defied the devil; the meandering Jordan where he was baptized; the ruins of the synagogue at Capernaum where he preached; the gentle hills where he gave us the Beatitudes.

Because the Bible is such an ancient document, it is not possible to be certain of all the "holy places," for some are not known and there are competing traditions concerning others. But even with this uncertainty my spirit is lifted by knowing I am in the general vicinity where a sacred event occurred. For instance, on World Day of Prayer, March 4, 1960, I went on the road outside of Damascus to the place where Saul the Jew of Jews was struck blind and told by God to cease persecuting the young Christian church. Fifteen feet below today's road are the arches and paving stones of the old Roman road. No one, of course, is sure of the exact spot where the Apostle was changed from persecutor to evangelist, but what his conversion meant for Christianity cannot be forgotten. Perhaps all of us may need to be blinded to our own personal goals so that our inner eyes can see God.

Before I went to the Holy Land, I assumed it was a place of ruins and half-reconstructed buildings. How wrong I was! The land of the Bible is vital and throbbing. The landscape, however, the rivers and mountains and flowers and grains are very much the same as when Jesus lived. So are the clothes worn by many of the inhabitants. Our Lord must have seen at least some of the structures which still stand, certainly the small mausoleum on the road from Jerusalem to Bethlehem which is revered as Rachel's tomb, the wall of Solomon's temple, the tower of Herod's temple, the pool of Siloam. Perhaps even some of the olive trees now growing in the Garden of Gethsemane are those under which Jesus prayed, as botanists say they may be over two thousand years old.

When I was in Nazareth in 1960, I found especially deep meaning in a visit to the home traditionally considered that of Jesus and his family. At that time the cave—for that is what it is—was not covered by a chapel, church, or convent. A previous structure had been torn down by the Franciscan fathers who planned and have since built a very large basilica there. I was fortunate to be able to walk directly into the small entrance of the cave as people did nearly two thousand years ago. It didn't really matter to me whether it was the exact abode of Joseph and his family, the cave is typical of Nazareth housing when Jesus was a boy.

There is an upper cave and a lower one, reached by a long winding tunnel which passes a huge rainwater cistern. The upper chamber could probably have been Joseph's workshop where he carved plows from olive wood. The lower chamber would have been the living area. It has wells for the storage of grain, a ventilating shaft for the fire, shelves for oil lamps, and a round outcropping of stone which could have been used as a table. Because they are below ground, the rooms stay at the same temperature the year round. Caves of this design are of great antiquity, some dating as far back as 2000 B.C. In many places in the world similar dwellings are comfortably inhabited today.

I also enjoyed my trip to King Solomon's mines at Elath on the Gulf of Aqabah at the southern extremity of Israel. The mines, from which gold, silver, copper, and iron were dug, and the smelters have been reactivated. Metallurgists have found that the winds which blow through the large natural contorted rock formations act as bellows in the smelting process. I have a brooch made of the polished ore which is veined, brilliant, and lustrous green.

Journeying through the Holy Land made me aware of the debt Christianity owes to Judaism. Our Bible was written by and about Jews. The Jewish patriarchs and prophets proclaimed that willful indifference and sin separate us from God who loves us. Through them God promised a Messiah by whose suffering we would be forgiven and saved from the consequences of our evil and sin. Jesus, the human son of God, the greatest man who ever lived, was a Jew. The New Testament is the record of the fulfillment of the promises given in the Old Testament. When Jesus said that he came not to destroy the laws, but to fulfill them, he meant the Jewish laws. Many Jews rejected Jesus, but after his resurrection he appeared to Jews, whom he commanded to be witnesses both in Jerusalem and in all Judea and Samaria and in all the earth. They were faithful, and it is through their courage and steadfastness that knowledge of Jesus was brought to Jew and Gentile alike. Some of my friends do not understand when I say, "I, too, am a Jew." I am a completed Jew, grafted onto the vine of Abraham, Isaac, and Jacob, accepting as my savior God's Messiah, the Lord Jesus Christ.

Petra

I had always longed to see the fabled abandoned city of Petra, the ancient capital of the Nabatean Kingdom. In Old Testament times it was the land of the Edomites, the descendants of Esau. The country was also known as "the land of Seir," its inhabitants were Horites, its capital, Sela. An important city on the South Arabian caravan route for several hundred years, Petra, the ruins of which survive today, reached its height at the time of Christ under the patronage of the Romans. Then, the territory of the Nabatean Kingdom extended as far north as Damascus; it was an agent of its king who tried to arrest Paul in Damascus. He escaped by being let down in a basket through a window in the city wall.

Petra lies in a wadi, aptly called the Valley of Moses because of the city's abundant supply of pure spring water. It is surrounded on three sides by precipitous cliffs of soft pink limestone and can be entered only by a narrow, easily defended defile.

I traveled from Jerusalem to Petra by car with two guides and an adventurous lady whom I had met in Jericho and invited to accompany me. When we reached the entrance of the defile, we changed to horses. So narrow is the rockbound trail that leads to the hidden city that I could touch both sides at once from the back of my horse. The passage is dark and shadowless; not even on the brightest days does the sun penetrate its depth. In many ways it reminded me of the chasm that leads to the Indian village on the floor of the Havasu Canyon. After threading and twisting our way for about an hour, we turned still another corner and suddenly, at the end of the dim corridor through a jagged cleft in the rock, we could see a rose-red Roman façade, bathed in dazzling sunlight. It was the Treasury, the most elaborate two-storied building in the city embellished with Corinthian columns, carved goddesses, pediments, and topped by a graceful urn all hewn directly in the living rock. Temples, roads, chariot arches, pedestrian arches, an amphitheater seating thousands of people, a monastery and many handsome tombs testify to the grandeur of the ancient city. There is evidence that some buildings were used as Christian churches as late as A.D. 447. But now all is desolate, sheltering only a few nomadic Bedouins and their goats. The judgments of Obadiah and Jeremiah have come to pass:

Now I am going to reduce you among the nations,
and make you utterly despised.

Your pride of heart has led you astray,
you whose home is in the holes in the rocks,
who make the heights your dwelling,
who say in your heart,
"Who will bring me down to the ground?"

Though you soared like the eagle,
though you set your nest among the stars,
I would still fling you down again—it is Yahweh who speaks.
                    Obadiah 1:2-4 (JB); Jeremiah 49:16

My companion and I toured the ruins and then played with some goats which a little Bedouin girl was tending. In the late afternoon a boy, who turned out to be her husband, brought a young goat which he offered for our dinner. I bought it and our guides butchered it and grilled kabobs made out of the leg flesh over the fire which we had made in the mouth of a tomb. The rest of the kid was boiled with rice in goat's milk and served in an earthenware dish made from Petra's pink clay. The rice and meat where heaped in a pyramid, and in the center of the white mass was placed the cooked head of the kid. Since I had bought the kid, the eyeballs, considered the greatest delicacy, were presented to me. Somehow I ate them; they were about the size and consistency of small rubbery grapes. Our guides and the Bedouins ate with us, all from the one dish, each using only three fingers in the approved Arab fashion.

While we were at Petra it rained, an almost unheard-of phenomenon in that region. On the return trip our car slithered in the deep, gluey mud, and the wheels spun to a halt. Nothing could move us. Finally our guides walked for three hours to get help. At last they returned with a camel to pull us out, but in a few miles we sank again to our hub caps. Happily a hospitable Bedouin man and wife took us two ladies into their hut for the night. The very young wife, who was expecting her second baby any minute, made an open fire in the middle of the floor and brewed us thick, sweet, Arabic tea. Then she brought an embroidered pillow roll out of a chest and put it on the floor for my friend and me beside the bed. After we were covered, her husband came in. We all slept, surprisingly with comfort, in the tiny but immaculate single room. During the night the Bedouins' three-year-old daughter crawled out of her parents' bed and curled up by my side. The only modern convenience in the hut was a small, battery-operated radio of which our hosts were very proud. The young wife had lovingly embroidered a cotton coverlet for it.

Jerusalem

From the fields around Bethlehem where shepherds still watch flocks at night, I like to look north to Jerusalem five miles in the distance. On clear days the golden Dome of the Rock shimmers in the sun. Sacred to the Muslims as the place where Mohammed rested during his journey heavenward, the building encloses a large rock many people believe to be the one on which Abraham nearly sacrificed Isaac. King Solomon built his great temple over it in the tenth century B.C., and it is thought that the stone was used as the high altar. Nothing of Solomon's temple remains today but some enormous rock slabs forming the western foundation. They are part of the "wailing wall," a place most holy to the Jews. The Temple Jesus knew was burned during the siege of Jerusalem by the Roman Titus in A.D. 70.

The Church of the Holy Sepulcher stands on a high point in Old Jerusalem, over an ancient Jewish tomb. Now mutually owned and uneasily shared by Roman Catholic, Orthodox, Armenian, Coptic, and Assyrian branches of Christianity, the present structure was built by crusaders in the Middle Ages. The original church was commissioned in A.D. 327 by the Empress Helena, mother of Constantine, the first Christian Roman emperor, to mark the place established by tradition as that of Jesus' burial. Each church group has its own procession around the elaborately carved marble sepulcher and conducts its service in its assigned area. The rituals are elaborate, the vestments rich with color, gold, and embroidery. Often the music of one group intrudes on that of another. The building is in extremely poor condition, owing to earthquakes and the divisiveness of its owners. Scaffolding put up in 1927 to shore the walls is only now being replaced as the needed repairs are made. Muslims have been appointed caretakers and guardians. They keep the keys and sleep inside the front door because the owners do not trust one another to manage the holy site.

Outside the city walls, to the north near the Damascus gate, is a hill one face of which is a cliff of shalelike rock. There are two small cave openings at the top of it, and a long thin opening near the bottom. At certain times of the day the sun and shadow make the cliff with its three apertures look like a giant skull. On its crest is a Muslim cemetery, covering an area known to have once been a place of execution. Some people believe this hill to be Calvary, the Mount of Golgotha, that is, the place of the skull.

About seventy-five years ago a tomb, dated to the first years of the Christian Era, was discovered at the foot of the hill. It is now called the Garden Tomb and through the years has gained more and more support as the place where Joseph of Arimathea and Nicodemus laid the body of Jesus.

Inside the tomb are two chambers: a mourners' room and an interior room in which a tomb-bed was carefully hand-hewn from the rock. Two other sepulchers were started but were not completed. The foot of the finished tomb-bed was crudely chopped to extend the length to accommodate a body longer than that for which it was originally intended. The Gospel tells us that Jesus was put in Joseph's newly made tomb where no body had yet been laid. High on the wall where it meets the ceiling of the tomb chamber is an opening cut at an angle to permit light to fall on the place where Jesus' body is believed to have been. Tombs are usually dark; the opening would have let in light by which Peter could have seen at once that the body was indeed not there.

Outside the sepulcher is a quarter section of a round stone disc which fits into a groove and which might have been used as the rolling stone to seal the tomb. On the wall above the door an anchor, an early Christian symbol, is incised. Still higher are two little niches in which Venus idols were found, testifying that the Romans felt this tomb sufficiently important to desecrate. There is also a cistern with fish, another Christian symbol, carved on its side, and the remains of an ancient wine press are near the tomb.

I have often stayed in the guest cottage in the garden close to the sepulcher and deep in the night, visited the tomb where Jesus may have rested before his resurrection. I have also sung the song "The Holy City" in the Holy City at a service beside the entrance to the Garden Tomb on Easter morn. Whether this is indeed where Jesus was buried is not of primary importance to me, for Christ is not in the tomb; he rose and is alive in the world today, ready to be with anyone who calls upon the name of the Lord.

On the Mount of Olives is a convent with chapel, marking the traditional place where Jesus taught his disciples the prayer we call "The Lord's Prayer." Inside the chapel and on esplanades outside, the familiar prayer appears in many languages on specially fired tiles. I talked so much about the chapel, Pater Noster, when I returned to Long Island that Eugenie longed to see it. We arranged for her to go to Jerusalem the next summer. When she found no prayer in her native Rumanian language, Eugenie and her friends collected money for three years to have the tiles made. Since the sisters at the convent were not allowed to correspond with the outside world, I agreed to speak to them about installing the tiles during my 1964 visit. Most of the wall space in the chapel and on the long exterior esplanades were already covered with prayer tiles, but to my amazement I found a vacant place at the right side of the altar. Eugenie's tiles in the Rumanian language can be seen there by pilgrims today.

CHAPTER EIGHT

Pain Is a Holy Angel

Journey to Rome

In 1969 I was invited on the Journey to Rome to attend the elevation of Archbishop Terence Cooke, head of the Archdiocese of New York, to the College of Cardinals. I had been introduced to the then Bishop Cooke at a luncheon given in New York by Francis Cardinal Spellman, with whom I was warmly acquainted for many years. That day I had taken Cardinal Spellman a copy of the American Bible Society's contemporary translation of the New Testament, called *Good News for Modern Man, The New Testament in Today's English Version*. Its clear, up-to-date language excited me and I wanted to share it with Cardinal Spellman because we had often talked about the Roman Catholic adoption of the vernacular for their services. He commented that a recent authorized version referred to Jesus Christ as "that fellow" and he felt that the translation could be improved upon.

Following the luncheon in the Cardinal's residence, we had sat in the corner drawing room, with the magnificently lace-curtained windows looking out on Madison Avenue and 50th Street. Cardinal Spellman asked me to read some of his favorite passages from the new translation. Sitting under an imposing portrait of Pope Paul VI, I read the verses. Cardinal Spellman was enthusiastic about the TEV. Every time I saw him afterward, he would tell me how much he was enjoying reading it.

When Cardinal Spellman died in 1968, I attended the mass the evening prior to the funeral. The congregation sang "A Mighty Fortress is Our God," the stirring hymn by Martin Luther. I sat in St. Patrick's Cathedral at the foot of the catafalque on which the Cardinal lay in state, thinking that God had brought us a long way through the maze of religious bigotry and misunderstanding dividing the church, and that the ecumenical spirit was indeed abroad in the world.

I had attended Bishop Cooke's installation as Archbishop. I have always found him sensitively aware of the changing problems of Christ's church today. In 1969 I was one of the Protestants invited to be a member of his party on the journey to Rome for his elevation to the cardinalate. About two thousand friends accompanied the four United States cardinals-designate. I had visited Rome many times before, touring churches, museums, and the Vatican. But of all my days there, I cherish most those of 1969.

We arrived in Rome on a Saturday in late April. Early the next morning I went to mass at St. Peter's Basilica to a special service for American visitors in the chapel of St. Jude. We were encouraged to sing lustily the great Christian hymn, "Praise to the Lord, the King of Creation," and the sermon centered on the little time we have as ours on earth to be of use to the Lord. There are no fixed pews in St. Peter's and only a few chairs, so that some of the congregation were kneeling, some standing, and some sitting as the priests blessed the sacraments, chanting, "Christ has died; Christ is Risen; Christ will come again." Communicants stood in three lines as they proceeded to the altar to receive the holy wafer. Then we all shook hands with our neighbors, saying, "Peace be unto you."

After the service I took the elevator to the roof of St. Peter's so I could have a good view of the Pope when he came out on his balcony to address and bless the crowds. I stood under the enormous statues of the saints which line the balustrade and look down on St. Peter's Square. Tiny yellow blossoms, somewhat like our dandelions, grew halfway up the knee of the last statue on the right end; he had what looked like a thunderbolt in his hand, but I don't know which saint he was. There are souvenir shops on the roof and a fountain which flows into an antique marble sarcophagus. Pilgrims were filling bottles of the water to take home.

After the Pope's appearance I climbed the three hundred tiny steps circling to the top of the great dome. The view of the crucifix-topped obelisk in the crowded square below, and of the gardens, the church domes and ruins of Rome beyond, made the dizzying ascent worthwhile, although it gave me a very painful stitch in my right side.

On Monday there was a ceremony at the Apostolic Chancery in which Archbishop Cooke received the *biglietto* or letter giving him formal notification of his elevation to the College of Cardinals. Tuesday was a free day. I went to a reception for the American delegation Wednesday evening and enjoyed the performance of singers and dancers in native Italian costumes. A man with a fine tenor voice sang Irish ballads. It reminded me of the many times my father had sung the same songs for our family and brought happy tears to my eyes.

On Thursday, May 1, I rose at 6:00 A.M. in order to arrive at St. Peter's by 9:15 for the Public Consistory at which Pope Paul would present rings to the new cardinals. Thirty thousand worshipers were present. The traditional long black dresses were not required, but I did wear my grandmother's black lace mantilla and the beautiful soft black doeskin gloves my beloved goddaughter, the gifted actress Virginia Kiser Storch, had given me as a bon voyage present.

There were bagpipers, ladies of the Holy Sepulcher, Knights of Columbus, Swiss Guards, and an expertly trained boys choir. The new cardinals came up to the high altar, two by two, genuflected, then turned and took seats in a semicircle in front of the Pope. The Pope blessed those on the four sides of the altar separately, then spoke and prayed in English, German, French, Spanish, and Latin. The choir sang gloriously and often. The cardinals, kneeling, received their rings from the Pope, and the service ended with the concelebration of the sacrament by the cardinals present with the Pope as the chief celebrant.

The ceremony was solemn and impressive, but much of the pomp and splendor of the past was muted by the modern trend toward simplicity. The Pope was not carried in the "sedia." Instead, he walked down the aisle with a quick, vigorous, buoyant, nearly bouncy step. There were no trains of watered silk, no ostrich-feather fans, no red slippers, no white fur capes, and no papal tiara. Most of the priests I spoke to, especially the younger ones, were pleased by these changes, for the feeling is that medieval embellishments lack relevance for the church's task in the world today.

On Friday the American group was honored with a papal audience, a surprisingly informal occasion. Each cardinal greeted the Pope with his own personal group of diplomats. One brought a little boy whom Pope Paul took on his knee and was photographed with. The Pope helped those presented to him from their kneeling positions, put his left hand on their shoulder or held their hands gently in his as he spoke to them. I was profoundly impressed by his enthusiasm, warmth, and openness.

In the late afternoon I attended a service at the ancient chandelier-lighted church of Saints John and Paul. It is one of the most ancient and most revered churches in Rome. This is Cardinal Cooke's titular church, as it was Cardinal Spellman's before him. Earlier it had been the titular church of

Eugenio Cardinal Pacelli before he became Pope Pius XII. As part of celebrating his first mass there, Cardinal Cooke sprinkled the doorway and floor and blessed the congregation as he walked by, the traditional ritual by which he takes possession of his special church. This beautiful service ended my sacred visit to Rome. It was one of the most moving and spiritually inspiring weeks I have ever had.

"O Death, Where Is Thy Sting?"

During the entire week in Rome I had, however, been quite physically ill. The pain that had developed in my side after my ascent to the top of St. Peter's on Sunday noon was soon accompanied by coughing and spitting of blood. I wondered if it were connected with a bout of pneumonia I had had the previous Christmas. Medicine which the doctors gave me had made it possible for me to be present at all the scheduled activities, but by the time I left Rome, I knew that I was very ill.

As soon as I arrived in New York, I was sent to the hospital. All three lobes of my right lung were congested, and so The New York Hospital became my home for the next six weeks. Because the medicine I had taken in Rome would have killed any pneumococcus, the doctors could not positively say I had pneumonia. They were equally uncertain as to whether I had tuberculosis, a giant blood clot, a pulmonary infarct, or a malignant tumor. I could take my choice. Meanwhile, pleurisy set in.

For weeks I was alone with an oxygen mask over my face, and with nebulizers to force moisture into my lungs to make breathing easier. Friends cheered me with small gifts and flowers even though no one was permitted to visit me. I remember the most elegant bouquet was from the prima ballerina Dame Margot Fonteyn. Margot is one of the greatest dancers in history; she is also among the most courageous and loving wives alive. Her husband, Roberto Arias, a Panamanian diplomat and newspaper publisher, was crippled in 1964 when political opponents had attempted to assassinate him. Theirs is a true "love story" of how love can triumph over political intrigue and physical disability. Margot's flowers reminded me of her stamina and gave me renewed strength.

May 16, 1969, was the day of greatest pain and best medical good news I have ever received. My physician, Dr. Claude E. Forkner, my close friend for many years, decided that I must undergo a bronchoscopy. This involved putting a metal pipe, eighteen inches long and an inch in diameter, with a mirror and a light on it, down my throat to examine first the larynx, then the bronchial tubes and finally the lungs. It hurt. How it hurt. The doctor asked me to cough as he probed. He said, "Larynx clear"; "left bronchial tubes clear"; "left lung clear." I was waiting for him to finish examining the right side. What a surprise when he said, "Right lung clear." Then the lung was flooded with liquid to rinse it out. As the pump went to work, suctioning off the fluid, I could feel the hardened mucus and blood ripping away from the air sacs in my lungs and the pain which I had known for weeks going with it. Thank you, God!

Of course I was relieved. I had not wanted to die, for we are always apprehensive about the unknown. But I felt cheated, too. God and I had had some glorious talks in my hospital room and I was prepared to meet Jesus face to face. And now here I was, left behind on earth to continue working for him!

I had many opportunities to speak of God in the hospital, talking with staff and nurses about why I reacted as I did. I had pain, but no fear. How could I have been frightened at the prospect of being translated immediately into the presence of my creator and redeemer, to dwell in his house forever, in fellowship with the throngs of believers down through the ages? I would have been reunited with my family and loved ones who had gone before. Our life on this earth is but for a little while. Though it is often filled with trials, if we believe in God and believe God loves us, we can face sickness or death, and rejoice in our infirmities, for God gives us freedom from anxiety about our final destination. Heaven is for eternity.

Whether I am a patient or a visitor in hospitals, I always carry literature—good literature which raises serious questions and gives answers about relationships with God. I give leaflets to people, leave them in waiting rooms, telephone booths, and rest rooms, and give copies of the New Testament to patients and staff. People in hospitals need to have reassurance about the love of God and a challenge to open their lives to his power, for everyone there is conscious of the possibility of death. During my 1969 stay at The New York Hospital, many nurses prayed prayers of commitment, and several student nurses, ready to graduate that summer, told me they intended to start Bible discussion groups in their new posts.

When we are desperately ill and do not die, we become aware of the extension of time God has given us, and we should desire to be of even greater use to him. I was thankful that in 1969 God gave me more time to serve him on the earth. The night before I left the hospital, I made a long "thank you list" which started with God's gift of life to me and included my dedicated doctors and nurses, my dear son Searle, my attentive goddaughter Virginia Kiser Storch, my capable, loving, and long-suffering secretary Noreen Gambeski. I listed also the great technical advances in science and medicine, the nourishing food, the farmers who raised the grain and the cattle, and the clean linens between which I lay. We are never able to list all our blessings for which we should thank God.

My son had called the evening following the bronschoscopy to ask how I was and to give me some welcome news. He had been waiting for the results of the test to tell me that he and Kathleen Gerard, an attractive, intelligent, artistically gifted girl he had known for several years, were to be married. Searle was then attending a leading eastern university from which he has since graduated with honors. He and Kathy are continuing their studies and I am so proud of them both.

Yet I could have made the same "thank you list" had I known that I was afflicted with a terminal disease. Dietrich Bonhoeffer, the German Lutheran pastor martyred by Hitler, once quoted a philosopher who said, "Pain is a holy angel, who shows treasure to men which otherwise remains forever hidden." Bonhoeffer, then in prison, went on to say that he was experiencing an incredible pain of longing for freedom and friends. Such pain, he added, must be overcome every time "and thus there is an even holier angel than the one of pain; that is the one of joy in God."

The deaths of loved ones, I think, are really the most genuinely painful experiences we have. But in finding our joy in God at such times we prepare ourselves for our own destiny. My father's death came in the early 1950s, after a long, useful, and fulfilling life—he was ninety-five years old. In 1963 my stepdaughter Gail died. At twenty Gail had married and was living in Sun Valley, Idaho. She was gloriously happy in the bright, crisp climate, the tree-covered, snowcapped mountains, and the world of nature she loved so much.

When Gail developed a persistent pain in her leg, the doctor in Idaho suggested she go to New York for tests. Specimens of bone marrow revealed that she had a virulent type of leukemia. The diagnosis came as a shock, for Gail was so active and so radiantly beautiful. She was told there was an imbalance in blood cells, and for two months we kept the truth from her. She came to New York at intervals for treatment. She stayed with my goddaughter Virginia, one of her school friends. Vicki's devotion and understanding gave her courage and many moments of joy during this difficult time.

Finally it was necessary for her to be admitted to Memorial Hospital for cancer patients. The structure of her blood vessels became so frayed that I could see great hemorrhages under her delicate skin. Gail asked all of her friends to give blood to the blood bank as she had had so many transfusions. She willed her beautiful gray-green eyes to the Eye Bank. Gail was buried near her mountain retreat in Sun Valley at the age of twenty-four. On her grave was a cluster of flowers with a single rose in the center, my parting gesture of love to the stepdaughter for whose happiness and life I would gladly have given my own.

My mother died on the last day of August, 1965, in Bradenton, just before her ninety-fifth birthday. About a year earlier it was necessary for her to have a serious operation. The prospect of her surgery was agonizing for me, but Mother took it quite calmly. She told me she was looking forward to meeting God and encouraged me to be strong. She comforted me, saying, "My darling, it doesn't matter to me if I go home on the operating table or later. I know where I am going to spend eternity and my bags are all packed."

Mother's spirits never dropped when she was confined to a wheelchair. She had an electric stair glide to move her between the two floors of her home, and she called it her "chariot" in which she "went up on high." When death came, Mother met it joyfully and confidently. Dr. Joe Blinco, an associate evangelist with Billy Graham, officiated at her "coronation" ceremony at the First Presbyterian Church in Bradenton. The following Scriptures, which reaffirm the claims of Christ and give praise to the Lord, were among those read during the service:

> Let not your heart be troubled: ye believe in God, believe also in me. In my Father's house are many mansions:

If it were not so, I would have told you. I go to prepare a place for you.

John 14:1-2 (AV)

. . . to be absent from the body, and to be present with the Lord.

II Corinthians 5:8 (AV)

And this is the record, that God hath given to us eternal life, and this life is in his Son.

I John 5:11 (AV)

The service ended with the jubilant strains of Handel's Hallelujah Chorus—"For the Lord God Omnipotent reigneth, forever, and ever, and ever, Hallelujah!" There was a second funeral service at the First Lutheran Church in Plymouth, Ohio, the church where four generations of our family had been baptized, confirmed, married, and buried. Mother was laid to rest next to my father and her parents in the Fenner family plot. Someday my coffin will join theirs.

Shortly afterward, my brother George died in Mansfield, Ohio. His service was attended by scores of friends and grateful patients, many of whom told me they were alive that day because of his great skill and devotion as a surgeon. I think often of a paragraph from Dr. P. B. Hills's *The Meaning of Death*, which reads:

> Our loved ones who have gone before us are safe and await our coming. The family circle is not really broken it is just enlarged. In Ephesians 3:15, Paul speaks of "the whole family in heaven and in earth." Right now some of our family are with us; some are in other parts of the United States or other parts of the world. In like manner, some of our family are here with us and some are in heaven.

Dr. Underwood's death in late 1969, in his early sixties, came after a year of illness. His homegoing caused a deep feeling of loss in the entire Westbury community. The year before, he had marked his twenty-fifth anniversary at the Church of the Advent. There had been municipal proclamations and a large reception. Both President Johnson and Governor Rockefeller of New York sent greetings. I visited Dr. Underwood in the hospital a few days before he joined the Lord. He could not speak above a whisper. "Eleanor, it isn't what you know here," he said, tapping his forehead, "it's what you've done here," touching his heart. "Keep on telling people how they can know Jesus." This was his deathbed command to me.

And that I have done—kept telling others how to know Jesus if they are facing death with no hope, and also if they are facing life with no hope. For a Christian, both living and dying are experienced in confident expectation that God's promises are true. Once in Oslo, Norway, I was nearly electrocuted when I tried to turn off two dressing-table lamps simultaneously when my hands were damp with hand lotion. I was facing a full-length mirror and saw myself turn ashen gray. I could not shake them loose and fell unconscious to the floor. The current was not strong enough to kill me, but it became abundantly clear to me when I recovered that we never know at what minute we may leave this life for a new home. I say, "Praise the Lord that Christ has taken the sting out of death for me and for all who take him into their hearts."

CHAPTER NINE

"I Work for the King"

"PTL"

A CHRISTIAN has a special source of joy, an inner radiance, as his life style. PTL—Praise the Lord! The born-again Christian who has received Jesus in his heart is transformed in his whole being; it is as if he has swallowed sunshine. The Holy Spirit of God really lives in him and controls, supports, illuminates his life. Even when there seems to be nothing but heartbreak and wretchedness, the turned-on Christian, like Job, can shout God's praises:

> I know that my Redeemer lives.
>
> 19:25 (RSV)

Or he can sing with the Psalmist:

> The Lord is my light and my salvation; whom shall I fear?
>
> 27:1 (RSV)

In other words, no matter what happens, we can always say, "Praise the Lord, anyhow."

The gift of the Holy Spirit brings new energy, new awareness, new freedom and creativity. And it is contagious. A true radiance cannot help but shine from one life to another.

It is stimulating to me that the fellowship of persons who have come alive in Christ is growing so vigorously. We are, I think, on the threshold of a mighty spiritual renaissance. Many, like myself, who were vaccinated by tasteful, do-good religion, others who were engrossed by their hot pursuit of worldly affairs, are now getting exposed to real Christianity and are coming down with real cases of God's love. And they are infecting others. They are spreading the Gospel, the Good News that God loves them and wants them to love him, now in this earthly life and for all eternity.

Many churches are catching the fever and are making Jesus' saving power central in their lives. The Rev. John Heuss, late rector of historic Trinity Episcopal Church at the head of Wall Street in New York City, wrote in *The True Function of a Christian Church*:

> It is a growing conviction of mine that no parish can fulfill its true function unless there is at the very center of its leadership life a small community of quietly fanatic, changed, and truly converted Christians. The trouble with most parishes is that nobody, including the Pastor, is really greatly changed. But even where there is a devoted self-sacrificing Minister at the heart of the fellowship, not much will happen until there is a community of changed men and women.
>
> . . . and within their little community [they will] reveal to others a kind of Christian relationship that is so different and so accepting that it cannot be resisted. That little changed community must be ever anxious to admit those who wish to share its life, whatever their race or condition may be. I can assure you that it is startling, indeed, to see how the most unlikely people are drawn to a real fellowship in Christ, when they see it for the first time.

Christianity has not failed; it isn't often seriously tried. The changed person or church sometimes brings division rather than unity and peace to the wider community. For Christian truth is not always popular with the world. If followers of Jesus are to be "light" and "salt," they must expect to be marked as different and to arouse a certain misunderstanding in their business, their professions, their social circles, their churches, even their homes. The cost of discipleship is great, but Praise the Lord, anyhow! Christians can pay that cost with joy and thanksgiving in their hearts.

We are a peculiar people.

> Christ . . . gave himself for us, that he might redeem us from all iniquity, and purify unto himself a peculiar people. . . .
>
> Titus 2:14 (AV)

We are different, set apart, unique. Some people may call us oddballs, but God intends us to behave in an unusual manner. We treat every man equally, whether he can be of use to us or not. We love our enemy, pray for him, bless him, turn the other cheek, even though he deals with us spitefully. We accept heartbreak, pain, and even death cheerfully and serenely. The world does not understand this. But unless we are recognized as different from other people, we ought to reexamine our lives, for it means that our Christianity isn't showing. Faith is like the wind. We cannot see where it comes from, we cannot touch it, but we certainly can see its results. A heart filled with faith blows freely into other lives.

Praise the Lord, too, that the Holy Spirit is at work in all sects and denominations, that the evangelistic movement is truly ecumenical. For the important thing is not the banner under which one worships, but the fact that one believes that Jesus Christ is God in the flesh, that he died on the cross so that all can receive his forgiveness, and that through him we can have absolute assurance of life with God, the father, in heaven for eternity.

A symbol I like to use for transformation is the butterfly because it has been transformed. Some people see these brilliantly winged creatures only as pretty ephemeral insects moving from petal to petal in fields and gardens. How much more they are! Butterflies are caterpillars—worms—first. They encase themselves in hard gray cocoons, and then they emerge as dazzling patterns of living beauty, soaring joyously in the heavenlies. They experienced new birth. I often wear a butterfly-patterned scarf or a butterfly brooch on my dress or hat. I attach them in odd places, on a hat brim, on my elbow, shoulder, or on a hemline, and when people ask why I wear them there, I say that butterflies are symbols of God's capacity to change us. Like worms locked up in cocoons, human beings can break out of the tight enclosures of selfishness, pride, intolerance, and indifference to God and like butterflies bring beauty and joy to themselves and to this world. As I've said before, Christ does not reform us, he transforms us radically. He wants us to change. And since we are not insects but human beings, we must actively and personally respond to Christ to be changed. Though we never know what God is going to bring in our future, we can say "Praise the Lord, anyhow" and by his spirit make whatever does happen an occasion of joy and thanksgiving.

I say "Praise the Lord" when I see adults and young people reaching out for new life in Christ, yearning for it, accepting it, and becoming persons who proclaim the truth of God's love. I say PTL for the increasing ease with which they talk openly and easily about their faith, and for the way in which old religious stereotypes are breaking down into a fellowship of the sons and daughters of God. The long, empty faces and cold, angry inner lives that belong to unrepentant and unforgiven people are disappearing. As Martin Luther said, "A singing person, a singing church is a real sign of the living spirit of the Lord." PTL!

"Up-and-Inners"

In 1957 I experienced God's transforming power. And as an awake Christian I have had to make fundamental, practical decisions as to how my life can best radiate the light and warmth I have in my heart.

Even after my divorce, I could still be considered a wealthy woman. The Bible says, I soon discovered, "It is easier for a camel to go through the eye of a needle than for a rich man to enter the kingdom of God" (Matthew 19:24, RSV), and "Go and sell what you possess and give to the poor, and you will have treasure in heaven" (Matthew 19:21, RSV). The widow who gave two copper coins, her all, at the Temple and received the highest praise of Jesus (Mark 12:42) made me think deeply about what I should do.

I know that many Christians have given away their possessions, and I seriously considered disposing of all of mine, too. But I found through studying and inquiring that good and wise stewardship is an important characteristic of a Christian's life in the world. It is a question of willingness to give everything to God. I use my home for God's work as a meeting place for Bible classes, conferences, teas and picnics, get-togethers of all kinds and for all ages. My own traveling, lecturing, and singing are never contingent upon a fee. Everything I have belongs to God. I am his steward and I do what I can to share my possessions and abilities for his glory.

Another practical decision I had to make was whether I was going to continue to live and work in the so-called "social" environment in which my married years were spent. As I grew spiritually, I became more and more aware that there are personal needs in drawing rooms of silk and tapestries and in ballrooms sparkling with jewels as well as in the parish halls and clubhouses of small towns or the slums of the cities. I used to think religion was fine for the "down-and-outers"—I now know the "up-and-inners" have just as many painful, agonizing fears and heartbreaks and they too are looking for solutions to their problems. There are opportunities for witnessing wherever there is human contact. I am ready for use as God's instrument at *any* time or in *any* place.

Wherever I go, I never fail to meet men and women who want to know about my Christian commitment. I try to be particularly sensitive to persons who ask carefully guarded questions about my faith and those who ridicule my commitment. Often both are trying to test my faith, hoping I have something unshakable which could make their lives more meaningful and secure. Often they are afraid and are reaching out for help and encouragement. Sometimes even at balls, receptions, and formal dinners, when people sit with me or ask me to dance, they look for an opportunity to share their gnawing inner struggles. They are hoping to find something in life they can believe in and cling to. I know that a few of my friends snicker about "Eleanor's religion." The more gracious just say "How quaint Eleanor is." Perhaps they would be more understanding if they knew how many of their friends, wives, husbands, and children have told me about the longing in their souls for true joy.

Once at a fashionable luncheon in the mid-1960s the hostess asked me to tell the entire table what I had been doing. I had not expected this request, for I had thought that those particular friends regarded my conversion as "going a bit too far." I told about my own spiritual transformation and about others whose lives had been given a new dimension by the transforming power of the Holy Spirit. I answered many of their questions, and when some asked how they could have this new life, I realized their interest was genuine.

We all joined in a prayer of commitment before we left the luncheon table, and the hostess started Bible classes for her friends, which continue even now after she has died.

A few years ago Louise Stewart invited me for luncheon.

She with her husband Jack owned Camelback Inn in Scottsdale, Arizona, the hotel-resort where Sonny and I stayed so often. Louise wanted to know what I had been doing since my last visit to Camelback. I told her and then took the risk of suggesting that maybe there were women among the guests who might like to hear about having a new dimension in life. She was understandably hesitant. Most people go to Camelback for fun and frolic rather than to study the Bible or hear an "evangelist." Perhaps because I had stayed there many months and had often sung for Camelback activities, Louise agreed to have me speak.

Our morning session was in a hot upstairs room. Only Louise and a few ladies, most of them elderly, came. But I could see that many of the women were moved by what I said about the importance of a personal relationship with God. Louise's life was changed. She has continued to have the discussion meetings, and a tiny chapel was built near the Inn for prayer, meditation, and quiet time with God. Her husband Jack also became an awake Christian. When, a few summers later, their daughter was killed in a Long Island automobile accident, they were able to accept the tragedy and it tested and strengthened their faith and trust in God. They continue to praise the Lord wherever they are.

I have seen the transforming power of Jesus at work among the down-and-outers, too. I have spoken and sung at the Salvation Army Harbor Light Center in the Bowery to men who have totally lost their direction in life, who can no longer face reality. Some of them were millionaires who are now living in flophouses because material riches alone could not give them strength to cope with the vicissitudes of life. Many men come to the center only for shelter and for hot soup and coffee, but some remain to make their commitments to Jesus, finding in a personal relationship with him the courage to start a new life. When I go there with Jerome Hines, the great basso-profundo of the Metropolitan Opera, we take turns; either he speaks and I sing, or he sings and I speak!

The street corners of the Bronx and the area under the Brooklyn Bridge are also gathering places for down-and-outers. I join fellow workers there, usually late at night, for then the junkies and the pushers and the prostitutes are milling around with no place to go, nothing to do. It is easy to speak to them separately or to attract a crowd. So many are in pitiable condition, their arms and hands covered with syphilitic sores and infections from unclean needles, their faces ravaged by dope, their bodies shaking with a bad trip or a fake fix. We offer to them the saving power of Jesus, who will stay with them always and help them to kick the drug habit "cold turkey." Even if they are noncommittal or antagonistic, we give them the names and addresses of rehabilitation centers so that when they say "Yes, I want to change today" rather than "maybe tomorrow," they will know where to go. Groups like Teen Challenge and Young Life and many churches have programs to train young people to be "soul winners" and to relate especially to drug addicts and dropouts. These programs are founded, first and foremost, on the heart-changing power of a personal Lord.

I Am Never Alone

Another question that I am frequently asked is why I have not married again. I think that marriage is the most beautiful complete relationship two people can have with each other, for marriage expands our awareness and sensitivity toward self and others, and provides a framework for the giving and receiving of love that exists in no other union. This is why God made man and woman. It is not surprising that the relationship of God to his people is so often expressed in the Scriptures by images of marriage.

For a marriage to be truly fulfilling each partner must give himself unreservedly to the other. This means that each must have something to give. When people who have no meaning in their lives marry because they hope that by "losing themselves" in another they will escape the emptiness of their own selves, their marriage will disappoint them. A marriage in which one partner or both partners are non-selves, is not a true marriage. Each must have inner resources and direction if the bond between them is to abide and grow.

Some people marry because of social pressure. This is particularly true of women. They feel that if they do not have a husband and children, society will consider them a failure. It is true that the most glorious occupation a woman can have is to make a home for a family, and that there are conventions which discourage her from tackling the world on her own. But the history of Christ's ministry overflows with accounts of single men and women who were able to bring Jesus to a far wider community, to succor and enrich it, than they could have if they had had the responsibilities of a home and family. A single person can lead an extraordinarily fulfilling life.

A few people, again particularly women, marry because they are afraid that if they do not, they will be unable to support themselves in the manner in which they want to live. A marriage for financial reasons is an empty and difficult marriage. It is really an extension of the marriage that is contracted because of fear of self. It signals lack of faith in God.

I have never looked upon marriage as a cure for loneliness. I am often lonely, but the aloneness that Christ has brought me is a beautiful aloneness. My son is grown and he and his wife have their own life. My mother and father, my stepdaughter Gail, and my brother have been "promoted to glory." I may be lonely, but I have asked God to come and live in me, and as he promised, he has sent his comfortor, the Holy Spirit. He is my constant help and support, with him I am never alone.

Today I find I can take advantage of my singleness to share

freely my love of Christ with others. But should I marry again, I would choose a mate who was first of all a true believer, for I think of marriage as a triangle whose apex is God. Each marriage partner occupies one of the base angles. As each grows closer and closer to God, the couple grow closer and closer together. In marriage, each should have love *beyond bearing*, the unqualified assurance that each loves the other, for part of love is sharing our joys and sorrows. When a sorrow is shared with someone else, it is halved; when a joy is shared, it is doubled.

Children of God

Since the middle of the century the world has been passing through chaotic times in politics, culture, and economics. Revolution has swept through the structures of society, and many traditional religious beliefs have been challenged or denied. Yet, I believe that this is a most exciting time for a Christian to be alive. Today there is a new sweeping of the Holy Spirit in evidence around the world. It is touching all religions and all denominations.

Young people, especially, have rejected past ways of thinking and acting. In many respects, my sympathies are with them—not with the drug culture or the drop-out culture or with campus riots or antipatriotism—but in their asking for changes, renewal, honesty, and reality in their concern for others. Their search for love, community, and a source of strength beyond themselves is at one with the great truths of Christianity. They know that worldly possessions are not a secure foundation for life. Their desire to fathom and to communicate truth makes them closer to the style of the original apostles than many lethargic and apathetic religious professionals. Their working to transform empty ritual and insensitive social or religious structures can be a God-oriented work. Our nation needs our young people as salt and leaven, and we should listen to them and encourage them.

By and large, young people today are the most dependable, intelligent, attractive, mature, articulate, concerned, and honest of any generation. I do not base this judgment on wishful thinking or reports in the press, for I am in touch with scores of young people constantly, through various organizations and my talks on campuses. My college invitations are not confined to church-related institutions. I am asked to speak at many of the more "radical" schools, and there, too I find many awakening Christians. I speak in lecture halls, dormitories, sorority and fraternity houses, in storefront academies and coffee shops, and to medical groups and music groups as well as church groups. I speak formally, or I hold rap sessions and even midnight curler sessions.

Whenever possible, I arrange question-and-answer periods and time for personal conversations after my campus talks. It is the same practice I follow in clubs, churches, prisons, or homes for unwed mothers. Reactions are the same everywhere. Some say, "Mrs. Whitney has gone off the deep end. She's wasting her time and money, it's all a drag." Others say, "Oh, I wish I could be sure. Maybe later I'll try Jesus." However, many young people are sorry for things they have done in the past and want to know if they can have forgiveness, if they can be freed from guilt and start a new life. They want inner joy and want to know if the Bible is true, and they pray a prayer of commitment and start on their new life as a child of God.

Others who know Christ ask how to read the Bible with greater understanding and how they can then share their faith with others. Now I have a new "tool" to suggest to them. In cooperation with the American Bible Society, I have written a commentary for a special edition of *Today's English Version* of the New Testament. Published in 1971, this edition marks key Scripture passages on the edges of the pages so they will be easy to find. It also contains several pages of explanatory comments on how to find and apply the New Testament's meaning to life and gives suggestions on how to share your belief and faith with others. The lettering on the cover is a vibrant pink color, and it is my hope that this marked edition will point many people to a vibrant, joy-filled life.

I know, from my work, that for every young person who has practiced violence, there are thousands involved in serious study on the campuses, and thousands who are working for God in para-ecclesiastical groups such as Campus Crusade for Christ, International Students, Inc., Inter-Varsity Fellowship, Young Life, Youth for Christ International, Fellowship of Christian Athletes, Navigators, and many church-affiliated youth groups.

It is reassuring that more and more, young people with long hair and "Jesus sandals" are effectively helping others counteract the drug habit, the trend toward superficial mysticism, and violent life styles. How do they do it? They wear the same clothes, use some of the same mottoes, and live in the same places as they did before they knew Jesus. The difference is that Jesus Christ is now at the center of their lives. He is their motivating power, and they want to share him with others. They go to the street corners, the coffee houses, the flophouses, and the beaches with Bibles in their hands and Jesus on their lips. "Do you know Jesus loves you? He'll help you." "Do you want to take a trip, man? Jesus is the real trip, and he'll never let you down." "Do you like the way you are? Jesus will clean you up."

I often think of a lovely girl who spent an afternoon at my home in August, 1970. We talked about Jesus and prayed together. After she went back to college she wrote: "Having been through journeys on LSD, peyote, and grass, I just want you to know that never have I been so 'high' as that afternoon at your home." Now she's sharing her faith.

And there was a college boy who had already been dismissed from several schools and was again facing suspension. His family were furious with him for wasting his time and their money. He was desperate when he came to me and said he really wanted to change, for he was disappointed in himself and ashamed of his behavior. He had tried hard to find a new direction for his life but did not know how to do it. We talked for some time about the healing power of God's forgiveness, and gradually that boy came to realize that if he truly committed his whole being to God he would become a new creature. He would see differently and act differently. And he accepted the fact that, although forgiven, he would have to suffer the consequences of his past actions. We read together Hebrews 12:11:

> God corrects us all our days for our own benefit, to teach us his holiness. Now obviously no "chastening" seems pleasant at the time: it is in fact most unpleasant. Yet when it is all over we can see that it has quietly produced the fruit of real goodness in the characters of those who have accepted it in the right spirit.
>
> (Phillips)

At last he prayed, asking God's forgiveness. He surrendered his will and told God he'd do anything he required. I arranged with the college to have him put on probation, and he took a full-time job to earn money for his tuition, going to school at night. His father, a leading businessman, scoffed when he heard that his son was praying and reading the Bible. He was sure that prayer would never help him and said, "I will believe it when he gets good marks and graduates." Two years later the boy graduated and with honors. He had learned to use God's transforming power.

I met Mary when she was a student at a junior college in South Carolina. She is a strikingly beautiful blonde and was voted the most likely to succeed in her class. She came to one of my talks in a church, and after my message, she prayed a prayer of commitment and asked Christ to take control of her life. In the time remaining before graduation, she started Bible discussion groups on her campus. Later she went on to the University of Tennessee in Knoxville. When on the first day she took her Bible out of the suitcase, her new roommate looked disdainfully at it and said, "By the way, I'm an atheist." That evening at dinner, after she had thanked God silently, she opened her eyes and saw that all the others at the table, including her roommate, had bowed their heads, so she prayed out loud. The girls asked her to talk to them about the Bible, and she started a study group in her room. Not long after, she was asked to report to the dean's office. "Are you conducting Bible study?" he asked. "Yes," she replied, thinking there might be a rule against it and that she was about to be reprimanded. "How wonderful," the dean continued. "For years we've been trying to start a faculty-student Bible discussion group. Would you help us form one?" She was also invited to speak in many churches and was an inspiration to young and old alike.

That summer Mary attended the training program of Campus Crusade for Christ at Arrowhead Springs, San Bernardino, California. There she met Barry Leventhal. Barry had been co-captain of the UCLA football team, a Rose Bowl hero, and he had a tough intellectual mind. When the claims of Christ were presented to him, he examined the evidence carefully and in time came to see that the promises made to the Jewish people in the Tanach are fulfilled in the Messiah, Jesus Christ. He became a complete Jew. For several years he worked with Campus Crusade, talking about the Messiah, Jesus.

During her second summer at Arrowhead Springs, Mary and Barry became engaged. They married and for two years worked together on the staff of Campus Crusade. Now they have a baby, Rebecca, and Barry, having decided to become a minister, is a student in seminary.

I am encouraged about modern young people because so many are asking early in life where they can find real meaning and purpose. They are not embarrassed, as I was when I was a teenager, about making a commitment to Christ. It is true that some are rejecting the formal religious patterns which leave them unfulfilled, but they are accepting Jesus Christ as their personal savior and are taking his commands seriously. They "go and tell the good news" enthusiastically and are loving their neighbors.

Let the Word of God Speak

I have learned many lessons in travel, not the least of which is the advice offered by the famous twelfth-century Jewish philosopher, Moses Maimonides, whose tomb I have often visited in Tiberias by the Sea of Galilee. "The highest form of charity," he said, "is to help a man to help himself."

This is the approach I think God wants us to use in presenting our savior, Jesus Christ. No one can force a man, woman, or child to make a commitment to God. We can help persons reach their decision by showing them how much God loves them and wants them to love him. We are the channels through which God speaks; it is his Holy Spirit that transforms lives.

I have tried to become a useful instrument of God, and since I travel a good deal, much of my witnessing is in airplanes. I no longer fly first class. Rather, I take a middle seat in the tourist section so I will have two persons with whom I can talk. I have a wonderful opportunity, since they can't open the door and leave! Naturally, I do not turn immediately to the passengers on the right and left and ask, "Are you saved?" All communication would immediately stop with that approach. But usually people who are traveling like to talk, and I try, guided by God's spirit, to be sensitive to my neighbor, to find the words that will move our conversation to his religious convictions in a natural way.

Only once in all my years has anyone said, when religion was introduced, that her faith was her own business and she didn't want to talk about it. The woman happened to be a jewelry buyer, and as I have designed some pieces of jewelry, we had pleasant small talk. It surprised me that in a short while she brought the subject back to religion and asked me about my faith. She never reintroduced her own religious convictions, but at least we terminated our journey as friends, and she had listened most attentively as I told my story. I explained that our first responsibility is to love the Lord our God with all our hearts and all our minds and all our souls; him only must we serve. Then we must love others as we love ourselves.

Perhaps a seed was planted. We must continue to sow the seeds of God's promises whether others accept them or not. And we must also water seeds already planted by encouraging ever-deepening study of the teachings of the Bible. And when we come upon a growing plant, we must fertilize and cultivate and shed sunshine upon it, talking of Jesus and joining in prayer. For nothing compares to the joyous privilege and responsibility of gardening for God, of opening hearts to the work of the Holy Spirit.

When I travel I carry a Mary Poppins-like satchel. This bag is covered with travel stickers from all around the world. It has become my identification, so that when I arrive at an airport, people meeting me often recognize me by it. Many times I have heard them shout, "Here comes the old bag now!" This "carryall" is especially intriguing to businessmen. It has been responsible for starting many conversations about faith, for they see it and say, "My, you travel a lot. Who do you work for?"

"I work for the king," I reply. Of course, my answer sounds strange. A typical reaction is "Oh, that's nice" or "How interesting," and the seatmate returns to his magazine. In a few minutes he invariably looks up and asks, "What king? What do you mean 'the king'?" Then I ask him who his king is. Some seatmates get the point. Others mention the president or maybe a governor. I urge them on, saying, "No, go a little higher." Usually what I mean is clear by then. "But lady, you don't look like a missionary to me," I often hear. But I am, and generally it does not take long to learn that the person next to me is a Congregationalist, Baptist, Quaker, Brethren, or belongs to the Assemblies of God or the Christian Church, or "used" to be this or that.

Many tell me about their churchgoing, the support they give to church projects, and what they are doing for the community hospitals, schools, city planning, and other civic organizations. Many are Churchians, who have confused Churchianity with Christianity, forgetting that although being busy in the church can be a sign of a Christ-filled life, it is not the basis or means of a personal relationship with him. We should work in our church programs and churches should be open twelve or more hours a day, every day as the Fenner Memorial Lutheran Church in Louisville, Kentucky, is. There they have classes in Bible study, music, art, and cooking, camping trips, and schools for unwed mothers. All churches need volunteers to wrap packages, knit, cook church suppers, and tend the altar; but a personal commitment to Jesus must come first. I think it would strengthen everyone's faith if at all functions and parties in the church one or two youths or adults told how God had given them a new life. And I wish ministers would ask one or two of their members to share at Sunday services every few weeks what Jesus means to them or when they knew they had firmed up their relationship to God. In churches where this takes place the congregation awakens with new vitality. So many churches are sleeping giants. Evangelism is the mainspring of an aroused living church.

So I tell my fellow airplane travelers how God changed my own life and gave it new dimensions. Then I ask them when they firmed things up with God. Some reply that they remember having done something of that sort long ago when they were little boys or little girls. I often suggest a prayer of reconfirmation and urge them to attend Bible discussion groups in their communities and to tell others about the change Jesus can bring in the heart of a man.

Once, coming back from Oregon on an airplane, I sat next to a sales manager of a lighting company. We had a small conversation in the course of which I told him I was traveling for the king. "Hurrummph!" he said. "If I get my kids to Sunday school, it's the best I can do." He picked up his briefcase and was immediately engrossed in reports and figures. So I took my Bible out of my "Mary Poppins" and started doing my daily lesson, using the outlines provided by Scripture Union. Soon luncheon came and we haltingly started another conversation which led to the transforming power of Jesus. I explained what had happened in my life and that God really loved him, too. By the time we landed at Kennedy Airport in New York, tears of relief and joy were streaming down his face. He had thanked God for forgiveness and asked him to take control of his life and make him a new man. I suggested he tell someone what had happened to him and he replied, "My wife will never believe me."

As he left the airplane he gave me his card—his name was Joe Rand—and asked me to write him. I sent him the Bible references we had read, together with the book *Now I Believe* by Robert C. Cook. I kept him and his family in my prayers. About six weeks later he wrote back, telling me he had attended a church supper which he had not done for twenty years. It was his first step in becoming an active member of his church. Then he accepted the job of financial chairman of the congregation. Joe has since attended counselors' training sessions, and has become Sunday school superintendent and chairman of the church board. He now serves as a lay reader. In his talk from the pulpit on Laymen's Sunday, he asked the congregation for commitment, participation, and involvement. Eighty percent of those present responded to his altar call.

I have visited Joe Rand and his wife Lil in their home several times, and they have arranged many speaking engagements for me. Lil and their four school-age children are also active witnesses for the Lord. Not long ago I had a letter from Joe, bringing me up to date on his family's work for Christ. He had just returned from Campus Crusade headquarters in California and was busy organizing a group from his community to attend one of the training institutes. He and his wife had recently attended an ecumenical weekend conference, during which he had witnessed and led an altar call. He is currently taking a correspondence course which will lead to a License to Preach and become a parttime Lay Pastor. I myself did nothing. It all happened because I was not afraid to tell my story and knew where to open the Bible and let the word of God speak to this man.

Invitation to Joy

To be able to help others receive God's gifts, to be in the presence of his transforming power, is the most exhilarating experience that I know. For when God fills a believer with his love, he gives him a new awareness, a new depth, a new strength, and a new joy that is rich beyond understanding. This new joy envelops his whole being in an iridescent network of shimmering gold.

When I first gave control of my life to Christ in 1957, I wondered if the inner transformation would be one of those mountaintop experiences that would fade away in the valley of shadows or the monotonous plains of daily living. But as I have grown in knowledge of God through living with him, my spirit has soared still higher. I have discovered that his promises are true and that his grace endures. Each day I am more conscious of the possibilities for the full and abundant life that are mine because I am his child.

This does not mean that my new life is without disappointment, discouragement, petty aggravations, and even heartbreaking sorrows. Rather, I know that even these can be turned into strengths when I surrender my will to God and let him take my burdens.

I still struggle with pride. How hard it is to admit that we have been wrong—to go to a person when we have been impatient, angry, foolish, or insensitive and ask forgiveness. Even when we are in the right, it spurs spiritual growth to apologize and to seek reconciliation. Nothing compares with the feeling of serenity that comes when the smothering weight of ill-feeling is shed and we have asked God to forgive, bless, and shower his treasure on those who have deeply hurt us. It takes imagination, discipline, and dying to the ego. But sustained by God's love we can do it. Even when others ridicule our desires to make peace and refuse to forgive us, our own spiritual periphery has been expanded.

Many people ask how they can have inner peace, joy, radiance, and assurance. Anyone can possess them—my own transformation is a testimony to the sure fact that God is faithful to the promises he made in the Gospel. Jesus said, "I am come that they might have life, and have it more abundantly." When we put our trust in God, we know that our lives will be guided in the way that is best for us, and that no matter what happens he will support us. Our fears dissolve and are replaced by steady, purposeful energy. Rather than withdrawing from them, we can face our problems openly and constructively. Throughout my own anguish and grief I say, "My God, I have you!" I do not like my ordeals and I am glad when they are over, but I tell God, "I'm willing to stay in these circumstances as long as you want me to. I'm willing to learn whatever it is you wish to teach me." I bear witness to the infinite loving care God has given to my life. Through him I have discovered reality so profound that it cannot be adequately explained. To those who have never experienced God no explanation is possible. To those who know the joy that comes from the abiding strength of the Father, no explanation is necessary.

Prayer is the lifeline to God. Every morning I wake up and say, "Good morning, Lord! I will praise you today." Whatever I am doing—driving, shopping, telephoning, cooking, writing letters—I send little shooting prayers to him, asking for his help and guidance. And I always make time for deep prayer. At night I thank him for all he has done for me and ask forgiveness for the mistakes I have made. God's love surrounds us all the time, but we must make contact with it if we are to receive its benefits. For a human being is like a beautiful lamp. It is not useful until it is plugged in to the source of light. Even then we must switch it on. We do this through prayer and conscious submission of our wills to his.

God is forever offering to us his gifts of reconciliation, forgiveness, and new life. It does not matter whether we are rich or poor, strong or weak, seemingly happy and content or miserable, in the prime of our lives or about to finish with earthly concerns. It is up to each one of us to accept his gifts and use them with all the strength of our minds and bodies. God longs for us to leave our fears and fretfulness and purposelessness behind and cross the invisible threshold into belief and partake of his light, warmth, and protection. He wants us to begin a new life with him, then everything we think or feel or do will reflect his glory. God is always by our side. We will have a life of radiant abundance when we accept Christ's loving invitation to joy, for he said,

These things have I spoken unto you, that my joy might remain in you, and that your joy might be full.